Progress in IS

Progress in IS encompasses the various areas of Information Systems in theory and practice, presenting cutting-edge advances in the field. It is aimed especially at researchers, doctoral students, and advanced practitioners. The series features both research monographs, edited volumes, and conference proceedings that make substantial contributions to our state of knowledge and handbooks and other edited volumes, in which a team of experts is organized by one or more leading authorities to write individual chapters on various aspects of the topic. Individual volumes in this series are supported by a minimum of two external reviews.

The Series is SCOPUS-indexed.

Lejla Turulja • Amer Celjo •
Mirjana Pejić Bach • Nijaz Bajgoric

Integrating ERP Systems and Knowledge Management

Improving Information System Adoption and Enhancing Business Performance

Springer

Lejla Turulja
School of Economics and Business
University of Sarajevo
Sarajevo, Bosnia and Herzegovina

Amer Celjo
Sarajevo School of Science and Technology (SSST)
Sarajevo, Bosnia and Herzegovina

Mirjana Pejić Bach
Faculty of Economics and Business
University of Zagreb
Zagreb, Croatia

Nijaz Bajgoric
School of Economics and Business
University of Sarajevo
Sarajevo, Bosnia and Herzegovina

ISSN 2196-8705 ISSN 2196-8713 (electronic)
Progress in IS
ISBN 978-3-031-68921-5 ISBN 978-3-031-68922-2 (eBook)
https://doi.org/10.1007/978-3-031-68922-2

This Springer imprint is published by the registered company Springer Nature Switzerland AG
The registered company address is: Gewerbestrasse 11, 6330 Cham, Switzerland

Foreword

The fundamental functions of ERP systems are in streamlining and integrating business processes and data across the organization and in enhancing organizational performances. ERP systems function as the foundation for knowledge management practices, which through increased operational effectiveness and decision-making capacity enhance organizational performance.

This book discusses new approaches in addressing ERP adoption, integrating ERP and knowledge management, and using them in improving organizational performances. Two methodological frameworks are used: TAM model and structural equations modeling.

Chapter 1 introduces the concept of enterprise resource planning from business information system perspective. A short literature review from three sources—(a) books/textbooks, (b) research articles, and (c) white papers—is given. The manuscript follows the concepts and frameworks introduced by Gartner (1990); the IS/EIS approaches defined in the textbooks written by Davenport (1998), Davis (2000), and Turban et al. (2010); and the EIS/ES works by Gunasekaran (2001, 2004, 2006, 2008, etc.) who extended ERP toward the concept of enterprise information systems and other enterprise systems such as agile/responsive manufacturing systems, supply chain management systems, and Industry 4.0.

The main part of the book focuses on ERP adoption (Chap. 2), relationships of ERP and knowledge management (Chap. 3), and the effects of ERP systems on organizational performances (Chap. 4).

ERP adoption process is of the greatest importance for companies or organizations implementing the ERP solution. Mostly used model—technology acceptance model is discussed as well as prior findings of the usage of this model in ERP adoption. Major critical factors studied in the chapter are top management, project management, change management, information quality, knowledge transfer, vendor selection, and effective communication.

The knowledge creation is supported by ERP through processing data using different modules. Knowledge conversion process is present and continuous through all of the stages. All four dimensions of knowledge conversion are used throughout the ERP adoption stages.

The authors argue that enterprise resource planning (ERP) systems are essential to increasing organizational capabilities and streamlining business processes in the ever-changing business technology environment. Key performance indicators can be greatly impacted by thoughtful alignment of ERP system integration with company objectives: Examining the impact of ERP system implementation on company performance, the conducted research revealed several limitations and offers suggestions for further research on this matter.

The book proposes a strategic ERP and KM synergy model consisting of four hypotheses and multiple hypotheses that assess the various interactions between enterprise resource planning (ERP) systems and various knowledge management (KM) practices within companies, thus highlighting their combined impact on company performance. Including both technical and organizational aspects that influence the efficiency of ERP, this model improves knowledge about its adoption and interaction with KM systems. The model suggests that ERP systems greatly improve some important aspects of knowledge management. The observed direct effects, such as the significant impact of ERP on the creation and generation of knowledge (KCG) and the use and application of knowledge (KUA), show that ERP systems are necessary in creating an environment suitable for innovation and efficient application of knowledge. Likewise, the favorable impact on knowledge exchange and transfer (KST) and knowledge protection (KP) underlines the role of ERP in enabling knowledge distribution and security within companies. Moreover, the model clarifies a direct positive relationship between ERP systems and company performance implying that ERP adoption can result in better operational efficiency and organizational results. This is particularly important because it offers real evidence for the strategic integration of ERP systems in promoting organizational success.

I strongly recommend this book for both researchers and practitioners in the area of enterprise systems.

School of Business Administration,
Middletown, PA, USA

Angappa Gunasekaran

Preface

The field of enterprise resource planning is truly multidisciplinary. It can be considered and analyzed from different perspectives such as organizational management, operations management, business information systems, enterprise information systems, enterprise systems, manufacturing systems, production systems, and systems integration. In addition, it can be seen as a concept, technology, application, system, and business philosophy.

This book explores the intricate relationships between enterprise resource planning (ERP) systems, knowledge management (KM), and organizational performance. By conducting a comprehensive review of the existing literature, this study proposes and presents two theoretical frameworks: the ERP acceptance model and the strategic ERP and KM synergy model. Their purpose is to provide clarity on the relationships between the three above-mentioned constructs. Empirical research has been conducted in specific settings, using purposive and convenience sampling methods as opposed to random sampling.

What is important to note is that the proposed models are fully supported and grounded in previously well-known theories. In this regard, the empirical validation aims to analyze the specific characteristics of the proposed links within the model as opposed to their overall predictive ability. Namely, certain relationships proposed by the models are supported by empirical evidence, while others lack such support. This highlights the complex nature of the interaction between ERP systems and knowledge management practices and the impact on business performance.

Given that both models are built on solid theoretical foundations: the first on the technology acceptance model (TAM), which offers insight into the determinants that influence the adoption and use of technological systems, serves as the basis for the ERP acceptance model.

The second, the strategic ERP and KM synergistic model, is based on the dynamic capability view (DCV), which clarifies how internal and external competencies are integrated, constructed, and reconfigured by strategic management processes to deal with rapidly changing environments. In other words, the book proposes two models that clarify the importance of ERP and KM for the business of organizations. Future research is recommended to examine these models in different settings to better understand their applicability and to determine how specific contexts affect the strength of model relationships. In other words, both models as a whole should be analyzed in different contexts, whereby the context will give priority to the strength of some connection, which will speak more about the context of the model itself.

Research of this nature is expected to provide a more complex understanding of the contextual elements that strengthen or weaken the benefits offered by ERP systems and knowledge management. As a result, a better understanding of how these elements interact in different organizational settings can be achieved.

We would like to thank Prof. A. Gunasekaran for his foreword.

A further special note of thanks goes to the managerial, acquisition, editorial, publishing, and marketing teams at Springer.

Sarajevo, Bosnia and Herzegovina Lejla Turulja
Sarajevo, Bosnia and Herzegovina Amer Celjo
Zagreb, Croatia Mirjana Pejić Bach
Sarajevo, Bosnia and Herzegovina Nijaz Bajgoric

Contents

List of Figures

List of Tables

Chapter 1
Enterprise Resource Planning: Information System Perspective

1.1 Introduction

The first chapter introduces ERP as a concept from the information system (IS) perspective encompassing the concepts of enterprise information systems (EIS) and enterprise systems (ES).

The term "Enterprise Resource Planning (ERP)" was first introduced in 1990 by Gartner to describe the next generation of Material Requirements Planning—MRP software. It aimed to integrate all business processes under one application (Jacobs & Weston, 2007).

Classification of the literature on ERP from IS/EIS perspective is divided into three sections: (a) books/textbooks, (b) articles, and (c) white papers.

The first section covers ERP concepts explained in the books and textbooks authored by the following authors: Turban, E., Davis, GB., Davenport, T, Laudon and Laudon. Other leading authors in the field of information systems, according to Google Scholar, such as Venkatesh and Gunasekaran are analyzed in the second section that covers research articles on ERP/Enterprise Information Systems. Venkatesh and his numerous articles will be mentioned in the chapter on EIS/ERP adoption, while Gunasekaran's work will be analyzed in the articles section of this chapter as he mainly published in journals and/or edited books dealing with Enterprise Systems, ERP, Supply Chain Management, Operations Management, Agile/Responsive Manufacturing, Industry 4.0.

The second section contains a short review of scientific articles published in peer-reviewed journals over the last 20–25 years, again an ERP-IS/EIS perspective is followed. Research papers published in the leading international journals are analysed. In order to create a framework for this book, ten themes are identified with a brief summary of the main articles that are written on these themes. This section is not intended at providing a detail description of the themes, nor a comprehensive literature review on ERP articles, rather, an attempt is made to present a "snapshot"

L. Turulja et al., *Integrating ERP Systems and Knowledge Management*, Progress in IS, https://doi.org/10.1007/978-3-031-68922-2_1

of the ERP phenomena from business computing perspective. Later in the main part of the book, as the book title suggests. We will be focusing on the aspects of ERP adoption, ERP and knowledge management and the effects of ERP systems on organizational performances. The following ten themes are defined for this section: ERP-Conceptual, ERP-literature review, ERP versus other enterprise systems (SCM/CRM/BI), ERP implementation—Critical Success Factors, ERP and Industry 4.0, ERP—Cases, ERP and BPR, ERP Adoption, ERP and Knowledge Management, ERP and organizational performances.

The third section contains the themes that are structured from white papers and similar sources and covers ten important aspects such as: ERP components, ERP Software selection, Using ERP, ERP and business transformation, ERP and BPR/TQM, ERP-Legacy systems integration, Customization, Industry specific applications, Education/Training, ERP success/horror stories. Although these documents are not scientific/scholar publications, the stories that they address help in understanding the ERP subject.

1.2 ERP in Information System Books

As the main framework of this book, the role of IT/Information System in modern business is defined according to the model presented in Turban et al. (2010), Davenport et al. (1998), Davis (2000) and Laudon and Laudon (2014).

Turban et al. (2010) used such an approach that positions information system as an organizational response to the requirements that exist in business environment. They developed the concepts of Business Pressures and Organizational Responses, with numerous pressures and technologies/systems explained. Business pressures include: Market pressures (Global economy and strong competition; Need for real time operations, Changing nature of the workforce, Powerful customers); Technology pressures (Technology innovation; Information overload); Societal pressures (Social responsibility, Regulation/Deregulation, Ethical issues). The concept of "Organizational Responses", according to this approach, contains several systema such as: Strategic Systems, Customer focus, Continuous improvements, Mass customization, Business alliances, E-business.

In their books on Management Information Systems, Laudon and Laudon (2014) created a framework for identifying the role of IT-systems with regard to business strategies, business processes.

With regard to the structure of ERP systems, both from the EIS/IS/ES conceptual and application perspectives, we follow the approach defined by Davenport et al. (1998) who presented the "anatomy of an enterprise system". He argued that "*Enterprise systems appear to be a dream come true. These commercial software packages promise the seamless integration of all the information flowing through a company—financial and accounting information, human resource information, supply chain information, customer information. For managers who have struggled, at great expense and with great frustration, with incompatible information systems and inconsistent operating practices, the promise of an off-the-shelf solution to the problem of business integration is enticing.*" In his model, Davenport et al. (1998) defined the general structure of an ERP system. As an example, he listed a set of components that belong to SAP suite:

Financials Accounts receivable and payable

- Asset accounting
- Cash management and forecasting
- Cost-element and cost-center accounting
- Executive information system
- Financial consolidation
- General ledger
- Product-cost accounting
- Profitability analysis
- Profit-center accounting
- Standard and period-related costing

Human Resources

- Human-resources time accounting
- Payroll Personnel planning
- Travel expenses

Operations and Logistics

- Inventory management
- Material requirements planning
- Materials management
- Plant maintenance
- Production planning
- Project management

Purchasing

- Quality management
- Routing management
- Shipping Vendor evaluation

Sales and Marketing

- Order management
- Pricing
- Sales management
- Sales planning

These components were parts of SAP package in the late 90s, more than 25 years ago. However, similar structure of a typical ERP package can be seen today, not only in case of SAP, but other ERP packages as well. The structure follows typical business functions such as production, sales, marketing, financial, accounting, human resources. What has changed in the last two-three decades are:

(a) application platform;
(b) methods of implementation,
(c) number and structure of "add-ins" and "add-ons"—additional applications/ modules such as CRM, SCM, decision support/BI.

Today's SAP solution, for example, one of them—for small and midsize companies—SAP Business One, includes the modules of accounting and financials, sales and customer relationships, reporting and analytics (www.sap.com/products/erp/business-one.html).

Another set of changes is related to the attributes of ERP-applications suite from application development perspective, with the following options: (a) standard client/server application ("thick c/s"), (b) Web-based client-server application ("thin c/s"), (c) ASP-based, (d) Cloud computing based. New ways of ERP implementation have been introduced as well. Some 25–30 years ago, almost all ERP implementations were "on-premise", with companies buying per-user licenses and paying significant amounts of money for ERP-implementation, mainly to "Big-Six" consulting companies (Arthur Anderson, E&Y, Delloite, PwC…).

The ASP model (Application Service Provider) introduced in the late 90s allowed using ERP packages "on remote basis", SaaS-based, Utility-based. Later, the Cloud Computing model was introduced and accepted as a predominant model of using ERP systems.

Davenport et al. (1998) argued that "… an enterprise system enables a company to integrate the data used throughout its entire organization" and provides a list of the main functions supported by SAP's R/3 package as a typical ERP application suite. He underlined the fact that Information Systems as an applied academic field must connect to practice. In addition, he created a well known syntagm "*Putting the Enterprise into the Enterprise system*" and underlined the fact that "*… if you are not careful, the dream of information integration can turn into a nightmare*". He noticed that Enterprise systems can deliver great rewards, but the risks they carry are equally great. However, the growing number of horror stories about failed or out-of-control projects should certainly give managers pause.

From the IS-conceptual perspective, Davis (2000) noted that "In North America, the terms information system (IS) and management information system (MIS) are identical in meaning and interchangeable in use. They refer to the system providing information technology-based information and communication services in an organization. These terms, and similar terms such as information management, also refer to the organization function that manages the system. … The academic field may be termed information systems (or IS), management information systems (MIS), information management, or management of information systems (MoIS). In other countries, there may be variations, such as informatics (often modified by organization, administration, or a similar term to differentiate from informatics as computer science)." Davis (2000) defined conceptual foundations of information systems as three approaches: an intersection approach that accepts any concept from any field if it appears to add insight and explanation to information systems practice and research, a core approach that seeks to define those ideas that characterize the discipline and make it distinct, and an evolutionary approach that seeks a cohesive set of concepts by combining the concepts from the core approach with concepts from other fields that over time are found to be especially useful to information systems. He defined a set of "*Underlying Disciplines for Information Systems and Concepts*": *Economics, Psychology, Sociology/Organization Behaviour, Communication, Decision making, System Concepts and Principles, Technology Acceptance/Diffusion, Management/Strategy, Information Concepts. In addition, he proposed a set of "Bodies of Concepts, Theories, Processes, and Applications Unique or Somewhat Unique to Information System"* and lists the following:

- Information system development concept
- Information systems management processes
- Information system development processes
- Information system development concepts
- Representations in information/communication systems
- Applications systems

Within this approach, ERP systems are classified into the subset of Application systems such as: Knowledge management, Expert systems, Neural networks, Decision support systems, Collaborative work systems/virtual teams, Group decision support systems, Telecommuting systems/distributed work, Supply chain systems, ERP systems, Inter-organizational systems, Organization communications systems: Internet, Intranet, e-mail, etc., Training systems, E-commerce applications, Customer support systems.

1.3 Articles: Information Systems Perspective

The literature on ERP from IS/EIS/ES perspective in terms of articles published in the leading peer-reviewed journals has been analysed with 150+ articles published in the last two decades (Table 1.1).

Ten themes are identified as follows:

1. ERP—Conceptual; IS/EIS/ES
2. ERP—Literature Review
3. ERP vs. other ES (SCM/CRM/BI)
4. ERP—Implementation: Methods and CSF
5. ERP and Manufacturing/Industry 4.0

Table 1.1 Classification of the ERP articles

Criteria	References
ERP—Conceptual; IS/EIS	Ash and Burn (2003), Alsène (2007), Davis (2000), Jacobs and Bendoly (2003), McGaughey and Gunasekaran (2007a, b), Møller (2005), Jacobs and Weston (2007), Romero and Vernadat (2016), Soffer et al. (2003), Lapalme et al. (2016), Benbasat and Zmud (2003)
ERP—Literature review	Addo-Tenkorang and Helo (2012), Ali and Miller (2017), Botta-Genoulaz et al. (2005), Darvish et al. (2015), Grabski et al. (2011), Gunasekaran et al. (2006), Haddara and Zach (2012), Moon (2007), Mukti and Rawani (2016), Nazemi et al. (2012), Ranjan et al. (2016), Schlichter and Kraemmergaard (2010), Coşkun et al. (2022)
ERP—Other Enterprise Systems (SCM, CRM, BI)	Gunasekaran and Ngai (2004), Gunasekaran et al. (2008), Gunasekaran et al. (2004), Hendricks et al. (2007), Holsapple and Sena (2005), Kuhn and Sutton (2010), Davenport and Brooks (2004), Akkermans et al. (2003), Ash and Burn (2003), Romero and Vernadat (2016), Grabski et al. (2011), Kuhn and Sutton (2010)
ERP—Implementation/ Critical Success Factors	Abd et al. (2017), Abdinnour-Helm et al. (2003), Akkermans and van Helden (2002), Berchet and Habchi (2005), Chou and Chang (2017), Da Silva and Rahimi (2004), Ehie and Madsen (2005), Finney and Corbett (2007), Krumbholz and Maiden (2001), Kwahk and Lee (2008), Mandal and Gunasekaran (2003), Mabert et al. (2003), Momoh et al. (2010), Motwani et al. (2005), Olson (2007), Saade and Nijher (2016), Soja (2006), Umble et al. (2003), Xue et al. (2005), Li et al. (2017)
ERP—Manufacturing; Industry 4.0	Alenizi et al. (2023), Gonzalez et al. (2024), Koh and Saad (2006), Senna et al. (2023), Kamble et al. (2019)
ERP—Cases	Motwani et al. (2002), Remus (2012), Rom and Rohde (2006), Sun and Bhattacherjee (2011), Tchokogué et al. (2005), Yusuf et al. (2004), Kirmizi and Kocaoglu (2020), Mukti and Rawani (2016), Coşkun et al. (2022)
ERP and BPR	Ng et al. (1999), Koch (2001), Subramoniam et al. (2009), Erkan (2009), Huq et al. (2006), Scheer and Habermann (2000), Cao and Rahmati (2005)
ERP—Adoption	Alavi and Leidner (1999), Alavi and Leidner (1999). Amoako-Gyampah and Salam (2004), Lederer et al. (2000), Chuttur (2009), Davis (1989a, b), Venkatesh and Davis (1996), Venkatesh and Davis (2000), Venkatesh and Bala (2008), Benbasat and Barki (2007)
ERP and Knowledge Management	Alavi and Leidner (2001), Alavi and Leidner (1999), Jennex (2007), Kuo and Lee (2009), Kecmanovic et al. (2003), Khalifa (2008), Magnier-Watanabe and Benton (2017)
ERP—Organizational Performances	Brown (2015), Byukusenge and Munene (2017), Darroch (2005), Hou (2014), Nicolaou (2004), Ruivo et al. (2020), Tarigan et al. (2018)

6. ERP—Cases
7. ERP and BPR
8. ERP—Adoption
9. ERP and Knowledge Management
10. ERP and Organizational Performances.

What follows is a short analysis of the first seven themes, while articles on ERP adoption, ERP and knowledge management, ERP capability and organizational performances will be analyzed in the chapters that follow. This analysis is aimed at positioning ERP systems within the context of business/enterprise information systems.

1.3.1 ERP: Conceptual Articles

In addition to the aspects discussed in the previous section, textbooks and monographs, conceptual papers on ERP and relations with IS/EIS can be seen in many research articles. We will mention some of them.

Romero and Vernadat (2016) argued that Enterprise Information Systems (EISs) are nowadays essential components of any enterprise system and can be defined as "software systems for business management, encompassing modules supporting organisational functional areas such as planning, manufacturing, sales, marketing, distribution, accounting, financial, human resources management, project management, inventory management, service and maintenance, transportation and e-business". They analyzed state of the art with regard to EIS and presented a brief history of Enterprise Information Systems, described various aspects of EIS such as EIS design and engineering, enterprise modelling, enterprise architecture, enterprise integration, enterprise networking. They shortly explained history of EIS indicating that Enterprise Information Systems history started with the introduction of computers in industry in the early 60s, using their computing and recording capabilities to automate manual tasks and to replace paper-based systems such as book keeping. Gradually, as the sophistication of computers, computer networks and database systems increased, EISs begun to take a more active role in supporting business processes, information flows, reporting and data analytics in organisations. Afterwards, in the 70s, the first Management Information Systems (MISs) appeared while other EISs started to support Material Requirements Planning (MRP) and a decade later, in the 80s, Manufacturing Resources Planning (MRP/II). The 90s gave born to Enterprise Resource Planning (ERP/I) packages, integrating databases and operational business functions in the back office and including support for human resources and quality management. In the 2000s, ERP solutions moved beyond enterprise boundaries to evolve to ERP/II, supporting the 'extended enterprise' and enabling inter-organisational collaboration embracing supply, design and engineering business functions. Nowadays, ERP/III aims at creating a 'borderless enterprise', supporting collaboration within the enterprise business functions and across the supply chains, including customers and the sales side of the marketplace.

The current trends on ICT technologies for enterprise information systems and main contributions to the generation of EIS are listed in El et al. (2016). According to these authors, ERP systems are now the backbone of the information system of any large organisation, however, a huge body of literature exists on the reasons of a poor level of "adoption" of these tools by their users.

Gunasekaran et al. (2004, 2006, 2008) considered enterprise systems in terms of the concepts, technologies, applications, including core ERP systems and Supply Chain Systems, combined with the fields of operations research and operations management. Consequently, ERP systems contribute to this aim by providing three different types of functionality:

- A transaction processing engine, allowing for the integrated management of data throughout the enterprise;
- Workflow management functions controlling the numerous processes flows that exist in the enterprise, such as the order-to-cash process or the purchasing processes;
- Decision support functions, assisting in the creation of plans (e.g., by doing an MRP run), or in deciding on the acceptance of a specific customer order (e.g., by performing an available-to-promise (ATP) check).

As a result, ERP adds the following business functionalities:

- ERP systems have replaced a myriad of old, undocumented, non-integrated legacy systems by state-of-the-art, integrated and maintainable software.
- ERP systems provide an enterprise transaction backbone that constitutes the glue between all kinds of best-of-breed solutions for specific processes or business areas
- ERP systems can be instrumental in transforming functionally oriented organizations into process oriented ones. The very nature of the ERP system forces one to think process-wise, rather than department-wise.

In addition, Gunasekaran et al. (2006) argued that Information technologies such as EDI, RFID, wireless, the Internet and WWW, and Information Systems (IS) such as E-Commerce and ERP systems have had tremendous impact in education, healthcare, manufacturing, transportation, retailing, pure services, and even war. Many organizations turned to IT/IS to help them achieve their goals; however, many failed to achieve the full potential of IT/IS.

1.3.2 ERP: Literature Review Articles

Research papers offering comprehensive literature reviews as a main research approach have been common in this area over the last two decades. Several authors approached their ERP research from this perspective by analyzing several dozens, even hundreds of research articles and provided new insights on ERP field. The researchers analyzed the papers published in the time periods from couple of years to several decades. Analyzed articles are mainly selected from the leading peer-reviewed journals indexed by WOS and/or Scopus.

Botta-Genoulaz et al. (2005) decided to primarily analyze the ERP-literature published in 2003 and 2004, on the basis of a classification according to six categories: implementation of ERP; optimisation of ERP; management through ERP; ERP software; ERP for supply chain management; case studies.

Moon (2007) defined the major themes in the ERP literature review as follows: (1) implementation, (2) using ERP, (3) extension, (4) value, (5) trends, and (6) education. With regard to ERP-implementation, he defined five sub-themes: (a) case study, (b) critical success factors, (c) change management, (d) focused stage, and (e) cultural issues. For "Using ERP"—theme, four sub-themes are defined: (a) change management, (b) decision support, (c) focused function, and (d) maintenance.

Schlichter and Kraemmergaard (2010) proposed new framework for conducting a literature review and used it for ERP research field. Abstracts from 885 peer-reviewed journal publications from 2000 to 2009 have been analysed and categorised into research discipline, research topic and methods used.

Ali and Miller (2017) found that top management support, good project management teams, and good communications are the top three most important critical successful factors during implementation. In addition, they found that research on pre and post-implementation is lacking, and that no industry standard implementation methodology has been developed.

1.3.3 ERP and EIS; Enterprise Systems (SCM, CRM, BI)

Several authors approached the field of enterprise resource planning from other enterprise systems perspectives, analyzing themselves structurally or implementation-wise, or considering aspects of integration with core ERP systems. The three modules or enterprise systems: Supply Chain Systems, Customer Relationship Management, Business Intelligence are addressed.

Gunasekaran and Ngai (2004) discussed information systems in supply chain integration and management and considered SCM as the twenty-first century global operations strategy for achieving organizational competitiveness. They argue that most of the SCM literature discusses only the implications of one or two aspects of supply chain such as strategies, tools and techniques. They found that a comprehensive survey of IT in SCM will be useful to identify the critical success factors of IT for an integrated supply chain.

McGaughey and Gunasekaran (2007a, b) explored the past, present and future of Enterprise Resource Planning. The article explores the evolution of ERP, the current status, and the future of ERP and argues that business needs have driven the design, development and use of enterprise—wide information systems. … While the concept of MRP was understood conceptually and discussed in the 1960s, it was not practical for commercial use. … In essence, MRP involves taking a master production schedule, inventory records, and a bill of materials and calculating time-phased material, component, and sub-assembly requirements.

1.3.4 ERP Implementation Critical Success Factors

Implementation aspects of ERP systems are in most cases considered with a certain number of critical success factors (CSF) that are defined by authors, either in general, or for specific industries or different implementation frameworks.

Ali and Miller (2017) found that existing research focuses predominantly on the implementation phase, but research on pre and post-implementation is lacking, and that no industry standard implementation methodology has been developed. Coşkun et al. (2022) provided an overview of ERP critical failure factors. They noted that ERP vendors are constantly telling their success stories on their web pages and in the magazines they publish. However, it is very important to analyze unsuccessful case studies and learn lessons from these cases in order to achieve success. There are enormous case studies in which the failures in ERP applications and the losses caused by these failures are explained.

Motwani et al. (2002) examined what factors facilitate or inhibit the success of ERP projects and compared a successful ERP implementation with an unsuccessful one.

Baykasoglu and Gölcük (2017) argued that although a successful implementation of an ERP project can deliver strategic competitive advantages, significant improvements in efficiency, productivity, and quality, enterprises encounter variety of difficulties in the adoption process. Unfortunately, many enterprises have reported ERP implementation to be fraught with failures due to the variety of challenges. Čeljo (2022) analyzed the articles on major factors in ERP projects and classified them into two groups: success and failure factors (Tables 1.2 and 1.3).

Coşkun et al. (2022) focused their research on ERP-failures and investigated the ERP failure factors that could help practitioners. They highlighted the ERP failure factors by using the SLM approach (systematic literature mapping which provided an overview of ERP critical failure factors (CFF). Li et al. (2017) investigated possible CSFs of an ERP system and analyzed the effects of CSFs from the perspective of IT governance.

Table 1.2 ERP adoption critical success factors (Authors' work)

Success factors	Author
– Legacy Systems – Business Vision – ERP Strategy – Software Configuration – Top management support – Client Consultation – Communication – Observation and feedback – Troubleshooting	Holland and Light (1999)
– Top management involvement and support – The requirement for a project champion – User training and education – Technological expertise – Process elaboration – Project team competence – Vendor support – Package selection – Use of steering committee – Business Process Reengineering – Use of consultants	Somers and Nelson (2001)
– Support from upper management – Project team expertise – Interdepartmental co-operation – Clear goals and objectives – Cross-departmental collaboration – Project management – Package selection – Change management – Vendor partnership – Vendor tools – Use of consultants – Steering Committee – Minimal customization – Architecture choices	Akkermans and van Helden (2002)

(continued)

Table 1.2 (continued)

Success factors	Author
– Technical compatibility – Perceived complexity – Business process reengineering – Top management support – Organizational objectives – Training – Competitive pressure	Bradford and Florin (2003)
– Project management – Reengineering business processes – User training and education – Technological infrastructure – Managing Change – Managing Risk – Effective Communication – Composition and teamwork – Consultants – User Participation – Goals and Objectives	Bhatti (2005)
– Defined objectives, aims, scope, and planning – Project team competence and organization – User education and training – Business Process Reengineering – Change management – Effective communication – User involvement – Project champion – Package selection	Sternad and Bobek (2006)
– Support from upper management – Communicating – Cooperation – Communication – Training – Technical Complexity	Bueno and Salmeron (2008)
– Top-level management support – Team composition and collaboration – Interdepartmental cooperation and communication – Establishing Business Plan and Vision – Project Management – Support from Vendor – Architecture choice – User Involvement – Software development – Business process reengineering – Legacy system – Deliverable dates	Kronbichler et al. (2009)

(continued)

Table 1.2 (continued)

Success factors	Author
– Top management support – Program on managing the change – Strategy for implementation – Business plan and vision – Project management – Importance of project team – Business process modelling – Software development – Legacy systems	Curko et al. (2012)
– Top management commitment and support – Project management – User education and training – Business strategy and vision – The infrastructure of the technology – Participation of departments – Change management – Communication	Al-Sabaawi (2015)
– Clear goals and objectives – Top management support – Involvement of end users – ERP system acceptance/resistance – Project champion – Skills, knowledge, expertise – Organizational culture – Well-balanced project team – Managing Change – Configuration of ERP system – ERP system evaluations – The ERP system's organizational fit – User training—Project management	Leyh (2016)
– Senior management – Vision and business plan – Enterprise and legacy systems – Reengineering Business Processes – Project Management – Change Management – The corporate culture – An enterprise resource planning system development – Consensus – User involvement – Implementation method and strategy – Objectives and goals – Resource availability – External factors	Hasan et al. (2018)

Table 1.3 ERP failure factors (Authors' work)

Failure factors	Author
– Failure to link technology plan to strategic plan – Failure to recognize need for business change – Misunderstanding organizational requirements – Failure in staffing project teams and sub teams. – Difficulty acquiring knowledge in software configuration – Changes to software or modification – Customizations that do not work – Failure to manage project scope – Inadequate intention for data clean-up – Failure to achieve normal operations – Data input errors – Consultants for product development and execution – Project personnel turnover – Issues with the shakedown phase – No growth of end user skills – Inadvertently reducing the scope of a project – Recognizing data quality issues and reporting requirements – Business disruption	Markus and Tanis (2000)
– Required information is not present – Organizational change – Culture issues – Technology infrastructure – Work processes are far from best practices	Hawari and Heeks (2010)
– On-time project delivery – On-budget project delivery – On-time delivery of expected functionality – Acceptability to the users	Baxter (2010)

(continued)

Table 1.3 (continued)

Failure factors	Author
– An ERP readiness evaluation was not conducted before project deployment. – Skilled end users frequently changed. – The organization's structure – Conflicts between organization and consultants – Conflicts between organization and vendors – Poor project management – Poor risk management – Lack of change management – Poor end user skills – Poor top management support – Poor business process reengineering – Lack of process oriented vision – Inaccurate data – The high system complexity	Amid et al. (2012)
– A lack of commitment from upper management – Ineffective user communications – Inability to gain user support—Inadequate project management approach – Attempts to create legacy application bridges – Dissensions among user departments – Project team composition – Failure to adopt a business process – Change requirements misunderstood	Huang et al. (2004)
– ERP system miss-fit – High turnover rate for project team members – Over reliance on customization – Poor IT infrastructure – Poor Knowledge transfer – Poor project management effectiveness – Poor quality of business process reengineering – Poor top management support – Too tight project schedule – User resistance to change – Unrealistic expectations	Yadav and Joseph (2020)
– Lack of understanding of organizational processes – Business process reengineering – High complexity of the system – Too much system customization – Vendors conflict – Cost overrun	Larasati et al. (2023)

1.3.5 ERP and Manufacturing Systems; Industry 4.0

With regard to the concept and technology of Industry 4.0, Kamble et al. (2020) argued that in the third stage of ICT adoption in SMMEs, the organizations use enterprise resource planning applications to automate and integrate their core business functions. The fourth stage represents the highest level of technological maturity with the SMMEs using digital networks and real-time decision-making systems. They developed a performance measurement system for Industry 4.0 enabled systems. Motwani, Alenizi et al. (2023) discussed the application of AI technologies in Industry 4.0 by reviewing 45 articles dealing with AI and Industry 4.0 integration. Their findings show that machine learning is the most common AI method for improving Industry 4.0 concept and technology. Gonzalez et al. (2024) considered the concept of Organization 4.0 within the trends of digital transformation by analysing the factors that are crucial on the realisation of this concept. They identified the roles of innovation, business intelligence and digital employees. The study revealed that innovation is a necessary antecedence for Organization 4.0. Koh and Saad (2006) analysed the factors that produce uncertainty of SMEs in the manufacturing sector that use MRP, MRPII and ERP systems in so-called ERP-controlled manufacturing environments. Kamble et al. (2019) discussed the practices of Industry 4.0 from the sustainable organizational perspective. According to them, Industry 4.0 refers to the digital manufacturing system provided by the successful integration of production processes, information technologies, and techniques. The primary objective of industry 4.0 is to improve the efficiency and responsiveness of the manufacturing system.

1.3.6 ERP Case Studies

Motwani et al. (2002) examined what factors facilitated the success of ERP projects as well as what actions can be taken to bring troubled ERP projects under control. Yusuf et al. (2004) identified key dimensions of implementation of ERP system within a large manufacturing company and identified core issues to confront in successful implementation of ERP system. Motwani et al. (2005) investigated the factors that lead to the success or failure of ERP projects and performed a comparative study of four firms that implemented ERP systems. Tchokogué et al. (2005) used a case study approach to study lessons learned from a successful implementation of an ERP project. A set of measurement indicators that were used to assess progress is defined.

Remus (2012) used case study to show external changes to ERP projects cab trigger a chain reaction resulting in weak performance. Rom and Rohde (2006) studied how ERP systems affect the ability to solve different management accounting tasks and analyzed the relationships between information system and managerial accounting, Kirmizi and Kocaoglu (2020) argued that when the failure factors in ERP projects are evaluated, the enterprises do not pay enough attention to ERP readiness and moved directly to implementation. They propose a novel ERP readiness assessment. Mukti and Rawani (2016) discussed the issues that are inherent to ERP projects when the company tries to switch from its legacy application to modern information system based on ERP. Coşkun et al. (2022) analysed several case studies that revealed that success rates of ERP projects are meager. They analysed different failure factors with varying perspectives for companies in different industries. Yusuf et al. (2004) discussed the EIS-ERP implementation as a case in Rolls-Royce.

1.3.7 ERP and BPR

Implementation of ERP/Enterprise Systems are often accompanied with BPR or TQM projects, before, together or later. Changes in IT/IS infrastructure are used as a tool for changing the way how business operations are performed. ERP packages are seen as best-practices—based business suites, therefore, the organizations that decide to implement them try to change the way they operate according to these best practices.

Business Process Reengineering (BPR) was developed by former MIT professor Michael Hammer, whose original Harvard Business Review article (Hammer, 1990) gave examples of the application of his technique. BPR is a major undertaking, it is frequently compared to surgery, hence, like every surgery, BPR may be risky. In medicine, there are alternatives and supplements to surgery such as treating patients with drugs. These alternatives are less costly, take longer time, or have to be taken constantly. Similarly, there are several continuous improvement programs that can substitute for or supplement BPR. Two such programs are just-in-time (JIT) and total quality management (TQM) (Turban et al., 2010).

Based on interviews with more than 200 companies, and 35 reengineering initiatives, Davenport and Stoddard (1994) identified seven reengineering myths:

1. The Myth of Reengineering Novelty: Reengineering, although about familiar concepts, is new in that these concepts are combined in a new synthesis. These key components have never been together before.
2. The Myth of the Clean Slate: Regardless of Hammer's (1990) exhortation: "Don't automate, obliterate!" clean slate change is rarely found in practice. Or, as Davenport and Stoddard (1994) state: A "blank sheet of paper" used in design usually requires a "blank check" for implementation.
3. The Myth of IS Leadership: In contrast to the much touted leadership role, IS is generally viewed as a partner within a cross-functional team that is generally headed by a non-IS project leader and a non-IS business sponsor who have better control over the processes that are being redesigned.
4. The Myth of Reengineering vs. Quality: Unlike Hammer and Champy's (1993) call for all out "radical change," most companies have a portfolio of approaches to organizational change including reengineering, continuous improvement, incremental approaches, and restructuring techniques.
5. The Myth of Top-Down Design: The implementation and execution of the redesigned processes depends upon those who do the work. Hence, the participation, and more importantly, acceptance and ownership, at the grass roots level is essential for successful BPR.

6. The Myth of Reengineering vs. Transformation: BPR is a process that contributes to organizational transformation (OT), however it is not synonymous with transformation. OT is defined as, "Profound, fundamental changes in thought and actions, which create an irreversible discontinuity in the experience of a system" (Adams 1984). OT is generally about the emergence of a new belief system and necessarily involves reframing, which is a discontinuous change in the organization's or group's shared meaning or culture. It also involves broad changes in other organizational dimensions besides the work processes: such as organizational structure, strategy, and business capabilities.
7. The Myth of Reengineering's Permanence: Davenport and Stoddard (1994) speculate that reengineering has peaked in the US in 1994 and would probably become integrated with much broader organizational phenomena: such as another synthesis of ideas that includes the precepts of reengineering; its integration into existing change methods; or its combination with quality and other process-oriented improvement approaches into an integrated process management approach.

According to Ng et al. (1999), in order to sustain a competitive edge in the global manufacturing era, enterprises need to adopt appropriate improvement schemes, two widely-used tools are ERP systems and Business Process Reengineering (BPR).

Koch argued that BPR and ERP are not necessarily complementary, but can, on the other hand, be designed support each other. Yusuf et al. (2004) stated that firms around the world have been implementing ERP systems since the 1990s to have a uniform information system in their organisations and to re-engineer their business processes. Erkan (2009) addressed the effects of BPR on ERP implementation and offered a comparative case study. Botta-Genoulaz et al. (2005) suggested the capturing of complete business environment in a business process reengineering (BPR) project with the help of information technology, thus the alignment of the standard ERP processes with the company's business processes is for a long time considered as a critical step of the implementation process. Subramoniam et al. (2009) addressed the role of BPR projects in the implementation of ERP systems.

1.3.8 ERP Adoption

Businesses today focus on investing in future IS projects to cut costs and improve their performance. The academic community was and will be increasingly concentrating on developing and testing models and theories to help the industrial sector predict systems use and save on investments. Various theoretical techniques have been used to investigate the uptake of information systems. In cognitive psychology, the theory of reasoned action (TRA) and the theory of planned behaviour (TPB) have their origins.

Fishbein and Ajzen formed a Theory of Reasoned Action (TRA) that analyses the relationship among perceptions, practices, attitudes, and behaviour. According to the theory, the behaviour of accepting the system is influenced by one's intention to act. This intention results from a person's attitude and subjective norm, namely, "the person's perception that most people who are important to him think he should or should not perform the behaviour in question" (Dillon & Morris, 1996). In contrast, TAM represents Management Information Systems (MIS) specific model that is developed from TRA. It is context-driven, and in case of the technology usage, social influences are not one of the determinants of behaviour (Dillon & Morris, 1996). Davis suggested in his thesis that three elements determine user motivation: perceived usefulness, perceived ease of use, and attitude toward using the system. The third component, the user's attitude toward using the system, is the most crucial determinant of whether the system will be accepted or rejected. Attitude towards use is the user's perceived level of desirability regarding the utilization of a particular technology. Davis also points out that two beliefs influence the user's attitude: perceived usefulness and perceived ease of use, which affects whether the user would utilize the system. Perceived usefulness represents the degree to which a user thinks that a particular information system would benefit them, for instance, enhance their work performance and assist them in being more productive and efficient. On the other hand, perceived ease of use is how users believe that actual usage would be uncomplicated and straightforward. The intention to use represents a level of likely outcome that an individual would use the system.

Even though other models have been employed in IS research, the Technology Acceptance Model (TAM) has been the only one to catch the IS community's attention (Chuttur, 2009). Working on his doctoral thesis at the Massachusetts Institute of Technology, Fred Davis proposed TAM for the first time in 1985. Later, Davis refined his model by adding variables and modifying the initial theory. Ultimately, TAM became the dominant theory in predicting and explaining the usage of the system.

Since the first version, TAM has been used widely in IS and IT research fields. It started with studies in the late '80 s and '90 s where TAM was used to predict computer and primary software usage (Davis, 1989a, b; Gefen & Straub, 1997). TAM has received empirical support via numerous studies from 2000 to 2010 (Venkatesh & Davis, 2000; Lederer et al., 2000; Koufaris, 2002; Mun & Hwang, 2003) used TAM in the areas of application usage, worldwide web usage, online consumer behaviour and web-based information systems. During years from 2010 until now TAM researchers continue to use TAM in social media usage (Carlos Martins Rodrigues Pinho & Soares, 2011; Rauniar et al., 2014). In general, TAM is a primary acceptance model used by IS researchers to examine external factors influence on main factors (attitudes and intentions) to use or adopt new technology. TAM has also been extensively used in the study of ERP acceptance as well as ERP successes and failures factors. Money and Turner (2004) used the TAM framework to analyse KMS adoption and discovered that the relationships between PU, PEOU affect systems usage. They also mentioned the previous TAM-based information technology acceptance research could serve as a baseline for knowledge management system adoption research.

1.3.9 ERP and Knowledge Management

Knowledge management helps people in an organization to communicate and share their knowledge. This fact guarantees the organization's success in competition with other organizations. Knowledge management systems (KMS) refer to information technologies to store, improve and distribute intra and inter company's knowledge. Knowledge management systems were presented as probably the most argued and polemicized subject in the knowledge management area. Even though knowledge management systems are not the crucial part of knowledge management, it is evident that all major players in the ERP industry have cloud and installation based KMS solutions that they integrate with their ERP modules. Davenport et al. (1998) describe knowledge management as the utilization and development of an organization's knowledge assets in order to achieve organizational goals. Burk mentions that knowledge management helps us to use appropriate information in the proper time for final correct decisions.

Authors give different definitions, but in general terms, we can say that knowledge management is the systematic management of an organization's knowledge assets to create value and meet tactical and strategic requirements. It is made up of initiatives, processes, strategies, and systems that support and improve information storage, evaluation, spreading, refinement, and formation. Knowledge management develops methodical strategies, projects, and practices to make, impart, and spread over knowledge in the company. Societal and specialized frameworks help knowledge management through serving companies to distinguish, select, obtain, stock, sort out, present, and use data to solve the problem, make a decision as well as for education, advancement, and strategic planning (Neumann & Tome, 2011).

A knowledge management system (KMS) is an IT-based system designed to support and improve knowledge management (Kuo & Lee, 2009). Today, many applications can be used in organizations by themselves or embedded in existing IS. KMS covers a number of applications made to properly store and use knowledge. KMS is built to use the tools to provide beneficial output to the organization or a person directly working in a specific part of KMS, typically called knowledge workers.

1.3.10 ERP and Organizational Performances

Enterprise resource planning (ERP) systems are essential to increasing organizational capabilities and streamlining business processes in the ever-changing business technology environment. Key performance indicators can be greatly impacted by thoughtful alignment of ERP system integration with company objectives.

ERPs are key tools for improving organizational capabilities, directly influencing business processes and performance results. An SLR approach was used in data collecting and study selection to better comprehend the relationship between ERP systems and organizational performance. The procedure of identifying studies and analyzing them in order to map the research area is described in Ch4.

1.4 ERP White Papers

The white papers are mainly published by ERP vendors, ERP implementation/consulting companies, and international organizations such as IDG, IDC, ITIC, CIO, SELECTHUB, TechTarget, Panorama. Numerous analyses and stories are published by ERP software vendors such as SAP, Oracle, Microsoft, and others, as well as ERP implementation vendors, consulting companies, other organizations.

The white papers cover several aspects of ERP systems such as:

1. ERP Components; Modules
2. ERP Software Benefits
3. ERP Selection—Buying ERP
4. ERP and BPR/TQM
5. ERP-Legacy Systems Integration
6. ERP Customization
7. ERP Industry Specific Applications
8. ERP Education and Training
9. ERP and Business Transformation
10. ERP Success Stories/Horror Stories

Both in its conceptual sense and as an integrated commercial suite, ERP systems have similar components (subsystems, modules). Most commercial suites available on the market today have the following modules; Financial, Financial Accounting, Purchasing, Marketing, Sales, Distribution, Human Resources, Operations, Inventory Management, covering basic business functions. In addition to these business modules, the suites include additional modules that are aimed at improving reporting and decision support, in terms of Reporting and Decision Support, Business Intelligence, Supply Chain Management, Customer Relationship Management modules. ERP software vendors such as SAP, Oracle, Microsoft, and others have similar structure of their ERP packages, offer similar methods of ERP implementation (On-premises, Cloud based).

Major benefits of ERP systems include: integrated solutions (instead of "island automation"), data integrity, data security, improved internal and external communication and collaboration, improved reporting and decision support, replacing legacy applications or integrating them with new platforms.

With regard to application platform, today's options are as follows: (a) On-premise, (b) Hosted, (c) Cloud. On-premise (On-Prem) solution is based on upfront purchases of the main components: servers, storage, server operating systems, database management systems, security solutions, applications or modules, accompanied with paying licensing costs, maintenance costs, update and upgrade, while hosted and cloud—based options are based on perpetual or subscription costs and hosting fees. All-in-one Cloud-based solutions.

ERP success stories are mainly published by ERP vendors, aiming at presenting cases in which their products and their implementations turned to be successful from several perspectives: implementation time (duration), financial/costs effects, user acceptance, improved performances, customer services, scalability and flexibility.

ERP disaster stories, failure stories or horror stories, such as those of Hershey, Vodafone, PG, Nike, HP, contain the stories about wrong/faulty implementations, implementation costs over budget, lengthy operational disruption, lengthy project duration, in general, negative financial effects for the whole business system. These stories are mainly written as white papers, newspaper stories, Internet portal-stories, not much treated in the scholar publications (research articles), however, even in that format are important for better understanding of ERP systems and their implementations. Several companies have admitted these kinds of problems, in some cases financial disasters, even well known international companies, however, many businesses and organizations in general that faced the kind of problems never admitted that. This underscores Davenport's (1998) note: "*Enterprise systems can deliver great rewards, but the risks they carry are equally great "... if you are not careful, the dream of information integration can turn into a nightmare"*.

1.5 Conclusions

This chapter introduces the concept of Enterprise Resource Planning and provides a "snapshot" of this subject from business information system perspective. A short introductory literature review from three sources: (a) books/textbooks, (b) research articles, and (c) white papers is given.

Our approach is in line with Davenport's philosophy "*Putting the Enterprise into the Enterprise system*" and his saying that "*Information Systems as an applied academic field must connect to practice*". In addition, we follow the concepts and frameworks introduced by Gartner (1990), the IS/EIS approaches defined in the textbooks written by Davenport et al. (1998); Davis (2000), Turban et al. (2010) and the EIS/ES approaches by Gunasekaran and his works published in journals and edited books (2001, 2004, 2006, 2008, …) who extended ERP towards the concept of enterprise information systems and other enterprise systems such as agile/responsive manufacturing systems, supply chain management systems, and Industry 4.0. An attempt is made to present a "snapshot" of the ERP phenomena from business computing (enterprise information system) perspective. Later in the main part of the book, as the book title suggests. we will be focusing on ERP adoption, relationships of ERP and knowledge management and the effects of ERP systems on organizational performances.

References

Abd, M. A., Nasr, E. S., & Geith, M. H. (2017). Benefits and challenges of cloud ERP systems: A systematic literature review. *Future Computing and Informatics Journal, 1*(1–2), 1–9. https://doi.org/10.1016/j.fcij.2017.03.003

Abdinnour-Helm, S., Lengnick-Hall, M. L., & Lengnick-Hall, C. A. (2003). Pre-implementation attitudes and organizational readiness for implementing an enterprise resource planning system. *European Journal of Operational Research, 146*(2), 258–273. https://doi.org/10.1016/S0377-2217(02)00548-9

Addo-Tenkorang, R., & Helo, P. (2012). Enterprise resource planning (ERP): A review literature report. *Lecture Notes in Engineering and Computer Science VO* – 2194, II(1), 1126.

Akkermans, H., & van Helden, K. (2002). Vicious and virtuous cycles in ERP implementation: A case study of interrelations between critical success factors. *European Journal of Information Systems, 11*(1), 35–46.

Akkermans, et al. (2003). The impact of ERP on supply chain management: Exploratory findings from a European Delphi study. *European Journal of Operational Research, 146*(2003), 284–301.

Alavi, M., & Leidner, D. (1999). Knowledge management systems: Issues, challanges, and benefits. *Communications of the Association for Information Systems, 7*, 2–41.

Alavi, M., & Leidner, D. E. (2001). Review: Knowledge management and knowledge management systems: Conceptual foundations and research issues. *MIS Quarterly, 25*, 107–136.

Alenizi, F. A., Abbasi, S., Hussein, A., & Masoud, A. (2023). The artificial intelligence technologies in Industry 4.0: A taxonomy, approaches, and future directions. *Computers & Industrial Engineering, 185*(October), 109662. https://doi.org/10.1016/j.cie.2023.109662

Ali, M., & Miller, L. (2017). ERP system implementation in large enterprises—A systematic literature review. *Journal of Enterprise Information Management, 30*(4), 666–692. https://doi.org/10.1108/JEIM-07-2014-0071

Al-Sabaawi, M. Y. M. (2015). Critical success factors for enterprise resource planning implementation success. *International Journal of Advances in Engineering & Technology, 8*(4), 496.

Alsène, É. (2007). ERP systems and the coordination of the enterprise. *Business Process Management Journal, 13*(3), 417–432. https://doi.org/10.1108/14637150710752326

Amid, A., Moalagh, M., & Ravasan, A. Z. (2012). Identification and classification of ERP critical failure factors in Iranian industries. *Information Systems, 37*(3), 227–237.

Amoako-Gyampah, K., & Salam, A. (2004). An extension of the technology acceptance model in an ERP implementation environment. *Information & Management, 41*(6), 731–745.

Ash, C. G., & Burn, J. M. (2003). A strategic framework for the management of ERP enabled e-business change. *European Journal of Operational Research, 146*(2), 374–387. https://doi.org/10.1016/S0377-2217(02)00556-8

Baxter, G. (2010). White paper: Key issues in ERP system implementation. *Large Scale Complex IT Systems*, 3–9.

Baykasoglu, A., & Gölcük, I. (2017). Development of a two-phase structural model for evaluating ERP critical success factors along with a case study. *Computers & Industrial Engineering, 106*(2017), 256–274.

Benbasat, I., & Barki, H. (2007). Quo vadis TAM? *Journal of the Association for Information Systems, 8*(4). https://doi.org/10.17705/1jais.00126. Available at: https://aisel.aisnet.org/jais/vol8/iss4/16

Benbasat, I., & Zmud, R. W. (2003). The identity crisis within the IS discipline: Defining and communicating the discipline's core properties. *MIS Quarterly, 27*(2), 183–194.

Berchet, C., & Habchi, G. (2005). The implementation and deployment of an ERP system: An industrial case study. *Computers in Industry, 56*(6), 588–605. https://doi.org/10.1016/j.compind.2005.02.009

Bhatti, T. R. (2005). Critical success factors for the implementation of enterprise resource planning (ERP): Empirical validation. In *The second international conference on innovation in information technology* (Vol. 110, pp. 1–10).

Botta-Genoulaz, V., Millet, P. A., & Grabot, B. (2005). A survey on the recent research literature on ERP systems. *Computers in Industry, 56*(6), 510–522. https://doi.org/10.1016/j.compind.2005.02.004

Bradford, M., & Florin, J. (2003). Examining the role of innovation diffusion factors on the implementation success of enterprise resource planning systems. *International Journal of Accounting Systems, 4*(3), 205–225.

Brown, M. M. (2015). Revisiting the IT productivity paradox. *American Review of Public Administration, 45*(5), 565–583. https://doi.org/10.1177/0275074014523102

Bueno, S., & Salmeron, J. L. (2008). TAM-based success modeling in ERP. *Interacting with Computers, 20*(6), 515–523.

Byukusenge, E., & Munene, J. C. (2017). Knowledge management and business performance: Does innovation matter? *Cogent Business and Management, 4*(1). https://doi.org/10.1080/23311975.2017.1368434

Cao, G., & Rahmati, N. (2005). BPR and ERP: A Chinese Case. *ACIS 2005 Proceedings*, 19.

Carlos Martins Rodrigues Pinho, J., & Soares, A. M. (2011). Examining the technology acceptance model in the adoption of social networks. *Journal of research in Interactive Marketing, 5*(2/3), 116–129.

Čeljo, A. (2022). *Technology acceptance model (TAM) based approach to adoption and use of integrated business information systems*, PhD thesis, University of Srajevo, School of Economics and Business in Sarajevo.

Chou, S., & Chang, Y. (2017). The implementation factors that influence the ERP (enterprise resource planning) benefits. *Decision Support Systems, 46*(1), 149–157. https://doi.org/10.1016/j.dss.2008.06.003

Chuttur, M. (2009). *Overview of the technology acceptance model*. Association for Information Systems AIS Electronic Library (AISeL).

Coşkun, E., Gezici, B., Aydos, M., & Kolukısa, A. (2022). ERP failure: A systematic mapping of the literature. *Data & Knowledge Engineering, 142*, 102090. https://doi.org/10.1016/j.datak.2022.102090

Curko, K., Stepanic, D., & Varga, M. (2012). Strategic and tactical success factors in ERP system implementation. *International Journal of Computers, 6*(4), 206–214.

Da Silva, R., & Rahimi, I. (2004). Issues in implementing CRM: A case study. *Issues in Informing Science and Information Technology, 1*, 1053–1064. https://doi.org/10.28945/799

Darroch, J. (2005). Knowledge management, innovation and firm performance. *Journal of Knowledge Management, 9*(3), 101–115. https://doi.org/10.1108/13673270510602809

Darvish, B., Naz, M., Nikpay, F., & Binti, R. (2015). A systematic literature review on enterprise architecture implementation methodologies. *Information and Software Technology, 62*, 1–20. https://doi.org/10.1016/j.infsof.2015.01.012

Davenport, T. H. (1998). Putting the enterprise info the enterprise system. *Harvard Business Review, 76*(4), 121–131.

Davenport, T. H., & Brooks, J. D. (2004). Enterprise systems and the supply chain. *Journal of Enterprise Information Management, 17*(1), 8–19.

Davenport, T. H., & Stoddard, D. B. (1994). Reengineering: Business change of mythic proportions? *MIS Quarterly, 18*, 121–127.

Davenport, T. H., De Long, D. W., & Beers, M. C. (1998). Successful knowledge management projects. *MIT Sloan Management Review, 39*(2), 43.

Davis, F. D. (1989a). Perceived usefulness, perceived ease of use, and user acceptance of information technology. *MIS Quarterly, 13*, 983–1003.

Davis, F. D. (1989b). Perceived usefulness, perceived ease of use, and user acceptance of information technology. *MIS Quarterly, 13*(3), 319–340.

Davis, G. B. (2000). Information systems conceptual foundations: Looking backward and forward. In *Organizational and social perspectives on information technology: IFIP TC8 WG8. 2 International Working Conference on the Social and Organizational Perspective on Research and Practice in Information Technology* June 9–11, 2000, Aalborg, Denmark (pp. 61–82). Springer US.

Dillon, A., & Morris, M. G. (1996). User acceptance of new information technology: Theories and models.

Ehie, I. C., & Madsen, M. (2005). Identifying critical issues in enterprise resource planning (ERP) implementation. *Computers in Industry, 56*(6), 545–557. https://doi.org/10.1016/j.compind.2005.02.006

El, S., Grabot, B., Thoben, K., Hribernik, K., Emmanouilidis, C., Von Cieminski, G., & Kiritsis, D. (2016). Current trends on ICT technologies for enterprise information. *Computers in Industry, 79*, 14–33. https://doi.org/10.1016/j.compind.2015.06.008

Erkan, T. E. (2009). BPR effect on ERP implementation: A comparative case study. *World Academy of Science, Engineering and Technology, 54*, 1513–1516.

Finney, S., & Corbett, M. (2007). ERP implementation: A compilation and analysis of critical success factors. *Business Process Management Journal, 13*(3), 329–347. https://doi.org/10.1108/14637150710752272

Gartner. (1990). *A vision of next generation MRP II*. Scenario S-300-339, Gartner Group, April 12, 1990.

Gefen, D., & Straub, D. W. (1997). Gender differences in the perception and use of e-mail: An extension to the technology acceptance model. MIS quarterly, 389–400.

Gonzalez, R., Gasco, J., & Llopis, J. (2024). Towards organisation 4.0. An empirical study. *International Journal of Information Management, 75*(June 2023), 102746. https://doi.org/10.1016/j.ijinfomgt.2023.102746

Grabski, S. V., Leech, S. A., & Schmidt, P. J. (2011). A review of ERP research: A future agenda for accounting information systems. *Journal of Information Systems, 25*(1), 37–78. https://doi.org/10.2308/jis.2011.25.1.37

Gunasekaran, A. (ed). (2001). *Agile manufacturing: The 21st century competitive strategy*. Elsevier, ISBN: 0-08-043567-X.

Gunasekaran, A., & Ngai, E. W. T. (2004). Information systems in supply chain integration and management. *European Journal of Operational Research, 159*(2 SPEC. ISS), 269–295. https://doi.org/10.1016/j.ejor.2003.08.016

Gunasekaran, A., Patelb, C., & McGaughey, R. E. (2004). A framework for supply chain performance measurement. *International Journal of Production Economics, 87*(2004), 333–347.

Gunasekaran, et al. (2006). Information technology and systems justification: A review for research and applications. *European Journal of Operational Research, 173*(2006), 957–983.

Gunasekaran, A., Lai, K. H., & Edwin Cheng, T. C. (2008). Responsive supply chain: A competitive strategy in a networked economy. *Omega, 36*(4), 549–564. https://doi.org/10.1016/j.omega.2006.12.002

Haddara, M., & Zach, O. (2012). ERP Systems in SMEs: An extended literature review. *International Journal of Information Science, 2*(6), 106–116. https://doi.org/10.5923/j.ijis.20120206.06

Hammer, M. (1990). Reengineering work: don't automate – obliterate. *Harvard Business Review*, July-August, 1990, pp. 104-I 12.

Hasan, M. S., Ebrahim, Z., Mahmood, W. H. W., & Rahman, M. N. A. (2018). Factors influencing enterprise resource planning system: A review. *Journal of Advanced Manufacturing Technology (JAMT), 12*(1 (1)), 247–258.

Hawari, A. A., & Heeks, R. (2010). Explaining ERP failure in a developing country: A Jordanian case study. *Journal of Enterprise Information Management, 23*(2), 135–160.

Hendricks, K. B., Singhal, V. R., & Stratman, J. K. (2007). The impact of enterprise systems on corporate performance: A study of ERP, SCM, and CRM system implementations. *Journal of Operations Management, 25*(1), 65–82. https://doi.org/10.1016/j.jom.2006.02.002

Holland, C. R., & Light, B. (1999). A critical success factors model for ERP implementation. *IEEE Software, 16*(3), 30–36.
Holsapple, C. W., & Sena, M. P. (2005). ERP plans and decision-support benefits. *Decision Support Systems, 38*(4), 575–590. https://doi.org/10.1016/j.dss.2003.07.001
Hou, C.-K. (2014). A model for evaluating the potential impact of integrating ERP systems with BI systems on organisational performance: An empirical study of the semiconductor industry. *International Journal of Technology, Policy and Management. Inderscience Enterprises Ltd., 14*(3), pp. 250–270. https://doi.org/10.1504/IJTPM.2014.062950. http://w3.bgu.ac.il/lib/customproxy.php?url=http://search.ebscohost.com/login.aspx?direct=true&db=edsdoj&AN=fb73014baa0591d69e7a7aed8e2f9f06&site=eds-live&authtype=ip,uid&custid=s4309548&groupid=main&profile=eds. https://doi.org/10.1080/10580530.2011.58558
Huang, S. M., Chang, I. C., Li, S. H., & Lin, M. T. (2004). Assessing risk in ERP projects: Identify and prioritize the factors. *Industrial Management & Data Systems, 104*(8), 681–688.
Huq, Z., Huq, F., & Cutright, K. (2006). BPR through ERP: Avoiding change management pitfalls. *Journal of Change Management, 6*(1), 67–85.
Jacobs, F. R., & Bendoly, E. (2003). Enterprise resource planning: Developments and directions for operations management research. *European Journal of Operational Research, 146*(2), 233–240. https://doi.org/10.1016/S0377-2217(02)00546-5
Jacobs, F. R., & Weston, T. C. (2007). Enterprise resource planning (ERP)—A brief history. *Journal of Operations Management, 25*(2), 357–363. ISSN 0272-6963, https://doi.org/10.1016/j.jom.2006.11.005
Jennex, M. E. (2007). *Knowledge management in modern organizations*. Idea Group Publishing.
Kamble, S., Gunasekaran, A., & Dhone, N. C. (2019). Industry 4.0 and lean manufacturing practices for sustainable organisational performance in Indian manufacturing companies. *International Journal of Production Research, 58*, 1319–1337. https://doi.org/10.1080/00207543.2019.1630772
Kamble, S., Gunasekaran, A., Ghadge, A., & Rakesh, R. (2020). A performance measurement system for industry 4.0 enabled smart manufacturing system in SMMEs – A review and empirical investigation. *International Journal of Production Economics, 229*, 107853.
Kecmanovic, D., Jerram, C., Treleaven, L., & Sykes, C. (2003). *Knowledge in organisations: A sense making view*. Retrieved from Warwick University papers. http://www2.warwick.ac.uk/fac/soc/wbs/conf/olkc/archive/oklc4/papers/oklc2003_cecez-kecmanovic.pdf
Khalifa, M. A. (2008). Knowledge management systems success: A contingency perspective. *Journal of Knoweledge Management, 12*(1), 119–132.
Kirmizi, M., & Kocaoglu, B. (2020). The key for success in enterprise information systems projects: Development of a novel ERP readiness assessment method and a case study. *Enterprise Information Systems, 14*(1), 1–37.
Koch, C. (2001). BPR and ERP: realising a vision of process with IT. *Business Process Management Journal, 7*(3), 258–265. # MCB University Press, 1463–7154.
Koh, S. C. L., & Saad, S. M. (2006). Managing uncertainty in ERP-controlled manufacturing environments in SMEs. *International Journal of Production Economics, 101*(1 SPEC. ISS), 109–127. https://doi.org/10.1016/j.ijpe.2005.05.011
Koufaris, M. (2002). Applying the technology acceptance model and flow theory to online consumer behavior. *Information systems research, 13*(2), 205–223.
Kronbichler, S. A., Ostermann, H., & Staudinger, R. (2009). A review of critical success factors for ERP-projects. *The Open Information Systems Journal, 3*(1), 14–25.
Krumbholz, M., & Maiden, N. (2001). The implementation of enterprise resource planning packages in different organisational and national cultures. *Information Systems, 26*(3), 185–204. https://doi.org/10.1016/s0306-4379(01)00016-3
Kuhn, J. R., & Sutton, S. G. (2010). Continuous auditing in ERP system environments: The current state and future directions. *Journal of Information Systems, 24*(1), 91–112. https://doi.org/10.2308/jis.2010.24.1.91

Kuo, R., & Lee, G. (2009). KMS adoption: The effects of information quality. *Management Decision, 47*(10), 1633–1651.

Kwahk, K. Y., & Lee, J. N. (2008). The role of readiness for change in ERP implementation: Theoretical bases and empirical validation. *Information and Management, 45*(7), 474–481. https://doi.org/10.1016/j.im.2008.07.002

Lapalme, J., Gerber, A., Van Der Merwe, A., Zachman, J., De Vries, M., & Hinkelmann, K. (2016). Exploring the future of enterprise architecture: A Zachman perspective. *Computers in Industry, 79*, 103–113. https://doi.org/10.1016/j.compind.2015.06.010

Larasati, S. D., Eitiveni, I., & Mahardhika, P. (2023). Analysis of ERP critical failure factors: A case study in an Indonesian mining company. *Jurnal Sistem Informasi, 19*(2), 34–47.

Laudon, K. C., & Laudon, J. P. (2014). *Management information systems: Managing the digital firm*. Pearson.

Lederer, A., Maupin, D., Sena, M., & Zhua. (2000). The technology acceptance model and the world wide web. *Decision Support Systems, 29*(3), 269–282.

Leyh, C. (2016). Critical success factors for ERP projects in small and medium-sized enterprises—The perspective of selected ERP system vendors. In *Multidimensional views on Enterprise information systems: Proceedings of ERP future 2014* (pp. 7–22). Springer International Publishing.

Li, H.-J., Chang, S.-I., & Yen, D. C. (2017). Investigating CSFs for the life cycle of ERP system from the perspective of IT governance. *Computer Standards & Interfaces, 50*, 269–279. ISSN 0920-5489. https://doi.org/10.1016/j.csi.2016.10.013

Mabert, V., Soni, A., & Venkataramanan, M. (2003). Enterprise resource planning: Managing the implementation process. *European Journal of Operational Research, 146*(SUPPL), 302–314.

Magnier-Watanabe, R., & Benton, C. (2017). Management innovation and firm performance: The mediating effects of tacit and explicit knowledge. *Knowledge Management Research and Practice, 15*, 325–335.

Mandal, P., & Gunasekaran, A. (2003). Issues in implementing ERP: A case study. *European Journal of Operational Research, 146*(2003), 274–283.

Markus, M. L., & Tanis, C. (2000). The enterprise systems experience-from adoption to success. *Framing the domains of IT research: Glimpsing the future through the past, 173*(2000), 207–173.

McGaughey, R. E., & Gunasekaran, A. (2007a). Enterprise resource planning (ERP): Past, present and future. *International Journal of Enterprise Information Systems, 3*(3), 23–3.

McGaughey, R. E., & Gunasekaran, A. (2007b). Evolution of Enterprise resource planning. In A. Gunasekaran (Ed.), *Global implications of modern enterprise information systems: Technologies and applications, information science reference* (pp. 17–32).

Møller, C. (2005). ERP II: A conceptual framework for next-generation enterprise systems? *Journal of Enterprise Information Management, 18*(4), 483–497. https://doi.org/10.1108/17410390510609626

Momoh, A., Roy, R., & Shehab, E. (2010). Challenges in enterprise resource planning implementation: State-of-the-art. *Business Process Management Journal, 16*(4), 537–565. https://doi.org/10.1108/14637151011065919

Moon, Y. (2007). Enterprise resource planning (ERP): A review of the literature. *International Journal of Management and Enterprise Development, 4*(3), 235–264.

Motwani, J., Mirchandani, D., Madan, M., & Gunasekaran, A. (2002). Successful implementation of ERP: Evidence from two cases studies. *International Journal of Production Economics, 75*, 83–96.

Motwani, J., Subramanian, R., & Gopalakrishna, P. (2005). Critical factors for successful ERP implementation: Exploratory findings from four case studies. *Computers in Industry, 56*(6), 529–544. https://doi.org/10.1016/j.compind.2005.02.005

Mukti, S. K., & Rawani, A. M. (2016). ERP system success models: A literature review. *ARPN Journal of Engineering and Applied Sciences, 11*(3), 1861–1875.

Mun, Y. Y., & Hwang, Y. (2003). Predicting the use of web-based information systems: Self-efficacy, enjoyment, learning goal orientation, and the technology acceptance model. *International journal of human-computer studies, 59*(4), 431–449.

Nazemi, E., Tarokh, M. J., & Djavanshir, G. R. (2012). ERP: A literature survey. *International Journal of Advanced Manufacturing Technology, 61*(9–12), 999–1018. https://doi.org/10.1007/s00170-011-3756-x

Neumann, G., & Tomé, E. (2011). The changing role of knowledge in companies: How to improve business performance through knowledge. *Electronic Journal of Knowledge Management, 9*(1), pp73–84.

Ng, J. K. C., Ip, W. H., & Lee, T. C. (1999). A paradigm for ERP and BPR integration. *International Journal of Production Research, 37*(9), 2093–2108.

Nicolaou, A. I. (2004). Firm performance effects in relation to the implementation and use of enterprise resource planning systems. *Journal of Information Systems, 18*(2), 79–105.

Olson, D. L. (2007). Evaluation of ERP outsourcing. *Computers and Operations Research, 34*(12), 3715–3724. https://doi.org/10.1016/j.cor.2006.01.010

Ranjan, S., Jha, V. K., & Pal, P. (2016). Literature review on ERP implementation challenges. *International Journal of Business Information Systems, 21*(3), 388–402. https://doi.org/10.1504/IJBIS.2016.074766

Rauniar, R., Rawski, G., Yang, J., & Johnson, B. (2014). Technology acceptance model (TAM) and social media usage: An empirical study on Facebook. *Journal of enterprise information management, 27*(1), 6–30.

Remus, U. (2012). Exploring the dynamics behind knowledge management challenges-an enterprise resource planning case study. *Information Systems Management, 29*(3), 188–200. https://doi.org/10.1080/10580530.2012.687309

Rom, A., & Rohde, C. (2006). Enterprise resource planning systems, strategic enterprise management systems and management accounting: A Danish study. *Journal of Enterprise Information Management, 19*(1), 50–66. https://doi.org/10.1108/17410390610636878

Romero, D., & Vernadat, F. (2016). Enterprise information systems state of the art: Past, present and future trends. *Computers in Industry, 79*, 3–13. https://doi.org/10.1016/j.compind.2016.03.001

Ruivo, P., et al. (2020). The relationship between ERP capabilities, use, and value. *Computers in Industry, 117*, 103209. https://doi.org/10.1016/j.compind.2020.103209

Saade, R. G., & Nijher, H. (2016). Critical success factors in enterprise resource planning implementation: A review of case studies. *Journal of Enterprise Information Management, 29*(1), 72–96. https://doi.org/10.1108/JEIM-03-2014-0028

Scheer, A. W., & Habermann, F. (2000). Enterprise resource planning: Making ERP a success. *Communications of the ACM, 43*(4), 57–61.

Schlichter, B. R., & Kraemmergaard, P. (2010). A comprehensive literature review of the ERP research field over a decade. *Journal of Enterprise Information Management, 23*(4), 486–520. https://doi.org/10.1108/17410391011061780

Senna, P., Barros, A. C., Bonnin Roca, J., & Azevedo, A. (2023). Development of a digital maturity model for industry 4.0 based on the technology-organization-environment framework. *Computers and Industrial Engineering, 185*(April), 109645. https://doi.org/10.1016/j.cie.2023.109645

Soffer, P., Golany, B., & Dori, D. (2003). ERP modeling: A comprehensive approach. *Information Systems, 28*(6), 673–690. https://doi.org/10.1016/S0306-4379(02)00078-9

Soja, P. (2006). Success factors in ERP systems implementations: Lessons from practice. *Journal of Enterprise Information Management, 19*(6), 646–661. https://doi.org/10.1108/17410390610708517

Somers, T. M., & Nelson, K. (2001). The impact of critical success factors across the stages of enterprise resource planning implementations. In *Proceedings of the 34th annual Hawaii international conference on system sciences* (pp. 10-pp). IEEE.

Sternad, S., & Bobek, S. (2006). Factors which have fatal influence on ERP implementation on Slovenian organizations. *Journal of information and organizational sciences, 30*(2), 279–293.

Subramoniam, S., Tounsi, M., & Krishnankutty, K. V. (2009). The role of BPR in the implementation of ERP systems. *Business Process Management Journal, 15*(5), 653–668.

Sun, Y., & Bhattacherjee, A. (2011). Multi-level analysis in information systems research: The case of enterprise resource planning system usage in China. *Enterprise Information Systems, 5*(4), 469–494. https://doi.org/10.1080/17517575.2011.610904

Tarigan, Z. J. H., Basana, S. R., & Suprapto, W. (2018). Enterprise resources planning project manager competency on improving organizational performance through process design and quality performance. In *ACM international conference proceeding series*. Association for Computing Machinery (pp. 153–157). https://doi.org/10.1145/3241748.3241777

Tchokogué, A., Bareil, C., & Duguay, C. R. (2005). Key lessons from the implementation of an ERP at Pratt & Whitney Canada. *International Journal of Production Economics, 95*(2), 151–163. https://doi.org/10.1016/j.ijpe.2003.11.013

Turban, E. et al. (2010). Information technology for management – transforming organizations in the digital economy, Wiley, 7th Ed.

Umble, E. J., Haft, R. R., & Umble, M. M. (2003). Enterprise resource planning: Implementation procedures and critical success factors. *European Journal of Operational Research, 146*(2), 241–257. https://doi.org/10.1016/S0377-2217(02)00547-7

Venkatesh, V., & Bala, H. (2008). Technology acceptance model 3 and a research agenda on interventions. *Decision Sciences, 39*(2), 273–315.

Venkatesh, V., & Davis, F. D. (1996). A model of the antecedents of perceived ease of use: Development and test. *Decision Sciences, 27*(3), 451–481.

Venkatesh, V., & Davis, F. D. (2000). A theoretical extension of the technology acceptance model: Four longitudinal field studies. *Management Science, 46*(2), 186–204. https://doi.org/10.1287/mnsc.46.2.186.1192

Xue, Y., Liang, H., Boulton, W. R., & Snyder, C. A. (2005). ERP implementation failures in China: Case studies with implications for ERP vendors. *International Journal of Production Economics, 97*(3), 279–295. https://doi.org/10.1016/j.ijpe.2004.07.008

Yadav, S. K., & Joseph, D. (2020). Prioritising critical failure factors for the adoption of ERP system using TOPSIS method. *International Journal of Operational Research, 39*(2), 145–159.

Yusuf, Y., Gunasekaran, A., & Abthorpe, M. S. (2004). Enterprise information systems project implementation: A case study of ERP in Rolls-Royce. *International Journal of Production Economics, 87*(3), 251–266. https://doi.org/10.1016/j.ijpe.2003.10.00

Chapter 2
ERP Adoption

2.1 Introduction

Enterprise Resource Planning (ERP) system provides software modules or applications to help businesses to perform daily activities and integrate their business processes. In order to remain competitive, organizations need to integrate business processes and share data with third-party providers and customers (Lee et al., 2003). Large and medium sized business started moving in late 90s from nonintegrated business applications to enterprise systems. Multinational companies use ERP to make their across the border operation easier since ERP can support various languages and comply with different tax laws, accounting principles and financial regulations. For the past decade also smaller companies are moving towards adoption of ERP systems due to availability of cloud solutions and renting applications from ERP vendors.

ERP systems can bring substantial benefits to a company. The most realized benefits of successfully adopted ERP are support for global operations, business process integration, data quality and integrity, real time reporting, quality and availability of decision making information and improved productivity. The success of their adoption relies on many different success factors. These success factors are studied by many researcher's in the information systems, management and computer science fields. ERP systems are of high importance in all industries since it serves as an operational and decision making backbone for businesses that adopted them.

Almost all positions inside the company will directly or indirectly deal with ERP inputs or outputs. Employees that directly use ERP modules need to be trained and motivated to use and adapt to ERP practices. Main concerns from the employee's perspective is what will happen to their job status and if their working routines will change. Difficulty in accepting the ERP best practices in some case can lead to

L. Turulja et al., *Integrating ERP Systems and Knowledge Management*, Progress in IS, https://doi.org/10.1007/978-3-031-68922-2_2

dissatisfaction and employee resistance to use the system. A company's success also depends on the appropriate utilization (Ibrahimović & Bajgoric, 2018).

Adopting ERP systems correctly and using appropriate approach to implement the system is of crucial importance for businesses. Implementation of ERP is studied from different perspectives and several approaches are currently used by vendors and consultants. Usually, companies use external companies and consultants to closely engage with internal team in order to implement ERP system.

There are several models/theories used in information system academic world to study adoption of new technologies.

2.2 Technology Acceptance Model Formation

Fishbein and Ajzen developed a Theory of Reasoned Action (TRA) in order to analyze the relationship between perceptions, practices, attitudes, and behaviors as well as their interrelationships. Based on the theory, there is a strong connection between accepting the system and an individual's intention to act in response to it. A person's intention is determined by the person's attitude and subjective norm, namely, the person's perception that most people of relevance to him think that he should or should not perform the behavior in question, depending on the situation (Dillon & Morris, 1996). According to the theory, beliefs determine attitudes towards possible outcomes and how they will be evaluated based on how they are perceived. TRA is based on a theory of information processing, according to which external factors only change someone's attitude if they change their beliefs.

As an extension of the Theory of Reasoned Action (TRA), the Theory of Planned Behaviour (TPB) was proposed (Yayla & Hu, 2007). Theory of Planned Behavior (TPB) is an extension of Theory of Reasoned Action (TRA), developed to provide better understanding and prediction of human behavior, especially in situations in which people have little control over their actions. Developed by Icek Ajzen in 1985, TPB has become a fundamental model in psychology and behavioral science. It analyzes the determinants of deliberate behavior. Both TPB and Theory of Reasoned Action study human behaviour by identifying and analysing the factors that influence a person's behaviour.

While other models have been used in IS research, the Technology Acceptance Model (TAM) has attracted much attention (Chuttur, 2009). The original technology acceptance model (TAM) developed by Fred Davis in 1986 represents a central approach to acceptance research. It assumes that two characteristics are crucial for users' technology acceptance: perceived usefulness and perceived ease of use.

Figure 2.1 shows that perceived usefulness and perceived ease of use are main determinants of attitude towards the using of new systems and further for behavioral intention to use the system and actual system use.

TAM 2, a more advanced version of TAM, was released in 1996. Venkatesh and Davis (1996) gave a final version used widely in IS research which focuses on the behavioural intention of the user to adopt information systems. Figure 2.2 shows the

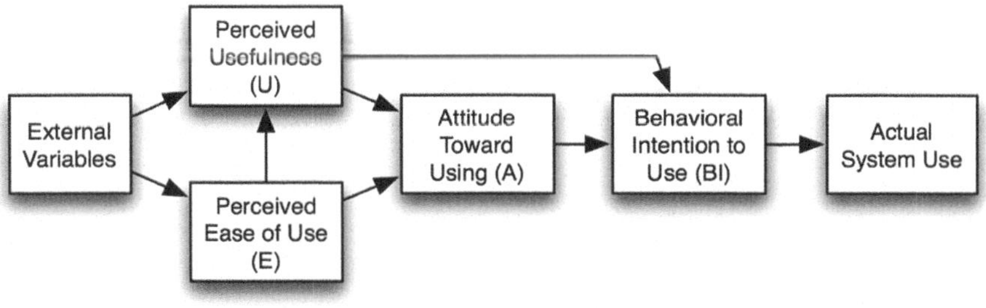

Fig. 2.1 Technology acceptance model I (Davis et al., 1989)

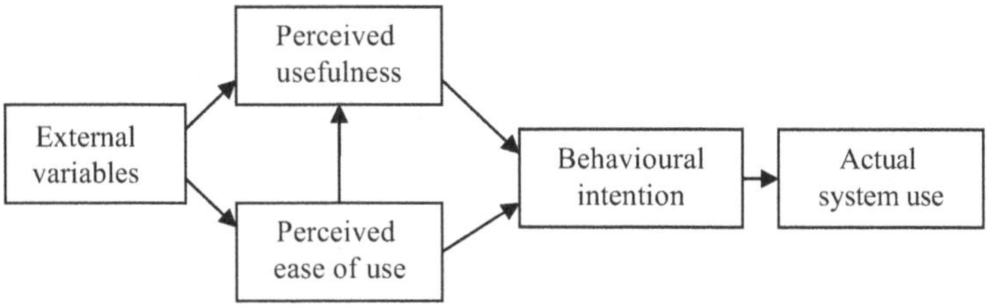

Fig. 2.2 Technology acceptance model II (Venkatesh & Davis, 2000)

continuation from TAM I where perceived usefulness and perceived ease of use are main determinants of behavioural intentions to actual use of the system. This model takes out attitude towards the using the system used in TAM I and shown in Fig. 2.1.

In TAM 3, authors introduced new relationships not tested before. External factor related to characteristics of the system, users experience, users feelings and quality of the data are proposed as determinants for perceived usefulness and perceived ease of use. These are determinants of perceived usefulness and perceived ease of use (Venkatesh & Bala, 2008). As shown in Fig. 2.3 subjective norm is also taken in consideration as determinant for behavioural intention and further for use behaviour of the system.

The Technology Acceptance Model (TAM) is widely used model for the acceptance of technology, including Enterprise Resource Planning (ERP) systems within organizations. The model uses the perceived ease of use (PEOU) and perceived usefulness (PU) as two primary determinants of an individual's intention to use a system. The TAM methodology has been successfully applied to a studies of acceptance of many technologies, including e-commerce, mobile services, online learning and healthcare information systems. Through the use of this service, organizations have learned how to better implement technological solutions by focusing on improving usefulness and ease of use to increase user acceptance and reduce resistance. In the context of ERP adoption, the TAM is used to test how different success and failure factors affect implementation and adoption. The following section provides some results and findings in relation how different success factors influence ERP adoption.

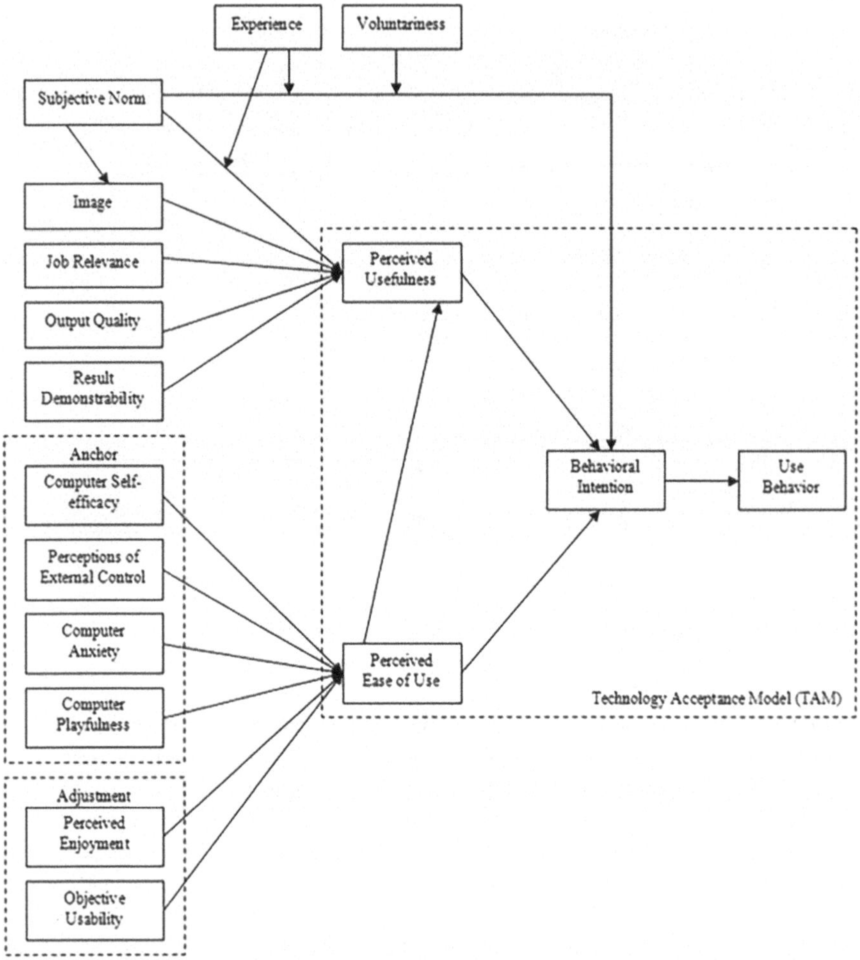

Fig. 2.3 Technology acceptance model III (Venkatesh & Bala, 2008)

2.3 Adoption Vs. Implementation

The ERP adoption process involves identifying the need for an ERP system, researching and evaluating different ERP solutions, and selecting the best solution. The process also involves assessing the organization's business processes, identifying the need to integrate or improve the system, and committing to the idea of integrating an ERP system to improve operations. The commitment to use ERP system is actually process of approaching all employees involved in the project and preparing them for actual use.

In the implementation process the ERP system is actually set up, configured, and deployed within the organization. Implementation involves project planning, software installation, data migration, system configuration, end-user training and testing. It is the 'how' phase, it involves ensuring that the ERP system integrates all departments and that employees are able to use it effectively. Adoption besides technical activities found in implementation process includes broad range of activities such as: change management, training, effective communications and software monitoring and evaluation. Implementation process is a subset of overall ERP adoption.

2.4 Applying TAM to ERP Adoption Critical Success Factors

Originally introduced by Davis in 1986, TAM has been widely applied across various types of information systems. The model's simplicity and robustness make it particularly appealing for researchers and practitioners seeking to evaluate the adoption of complex systems like ERP. ERP systems integrate internal and external processes across an entire organization. Understanding factors that influence ERP acceptance is crucial for ensuring successful adoption and utilization. In order to understand ERP adoption process we need to understand user perceptions about using ERP system. From the vendor side we need to provide ongoing effort to improve fit between ERP system and our client needs.

In order to understand and predict how users will adopt and use ERP systems, the TAM's core principles—Perceived Usefulness (PU) and Perceived Ease of Use (PEOU)—are applied.

- **Perceived Usefulness (PU)**—In the TAM context, perceived usefulness refers to the degree to which a person believes that using a particular system would enhance their job performance (Davis, 1985). For ERP systems Perceived usefulness represents the degree to which an end user thinks that a particular ERP module or function would benefit them, improve their work performance and assist them in being more productive and efficient. Organizations aiming to enhance ERP adoption should, therefore, focus on receiving the tangible benefits that these systems can offer to end users.
- **Perceived Ease of Use (PEOU)**—Perceived ease of use is the degree to which a person believes that using a particular system would be free of effort (Davis, 1985). Perceived ease of use is how users believe that actual usage of ERP modules would be uncomplicated and straightforward.
- This aspect is particularly critical for ERP systems, which are often perceived as complex and difficult to adopt. Simplifying the user interface, providing comprehensive training, and ensuring adequate support can making the system more approachable and easier to adopt.
- **Behavioral Intention (BI)**—Behavioral intention to use a system refers to an individual's perceived behavior regarding the use of a particular system, such as software or set of applications. From the ERP adoption perspective this can be

translated that ERP modules are relevant to user's needs and that they have adequate support and trainings to build their motivation to use the ERP modules.

While TAM provides a strong starting point, studying ERP acceptance involves considering external factors that could influence PU, PEOU and BI. ERP systems are complex and involve multiple and diverse groups of users such as top managers, middle managers, task workers and technicians. External factors such as: organizational knowledge sharing culture, change management processes, project management, top management involvement are aspects that are not explicitly accounted for in the original TAM and can significantly influence ERP adoption. In Chap. 1, Tables 1.2 and 1.3, many success and failure factors are summarized from previous studies that should be taken in consideration for adoption of ERP. As many authors findings suggested most important success factors for ERP implementation are: top management support, project management, change management, ERP selection, integration and configuration of ERP, end user training ERP system support, execution team and knowledge transfer. Al-Fawaz et al. (2010), Celjo (2022), Umble et al. (2003), Nah and Delgado (2006), Loh and Koh (2004), Somers and Nelson (2004). Figure 2.4 summarizes most important adoption success factors found in the literature.

The following section will provide insights on some literature findings in relations to these critical success factors. Different authors studied relationship of these factors to the main TAM constructs and overall system adoption. Short findings are discussed below.

Top Management Support—It is the responsibility of top management to identify ERP system implementation challenges even before the project starts, promote innovation in order to increase willingness to accept new system (Leyh, 2016), and monitor activities of different departments inside the company (Verma & Kumar, 2013). In addition to providing guidance, the top management supports the implementation of ERP by providing resources (Bhatti, 2005). Dantes and Hasibuan state top management should establish clear ERP implementation goals and visions. Clear goals will ensure that project phase's deadlines are met and implementation strategy developed. Leyh (2016) states that the promotion of innovation by top management will increase workers' willingness to accept the innovations. Hancerliogullari and Damar (2022) used expended TAM to investigate different factors in SAP usage in Turkey. They found that top management support and internal SAP consultant engagement are closely related with user satisfaction to use the SAP ERP systems. Their results show that PEU is greatly impacted by SAP consultant support. Importance of top management support is essential especially in providing resources to integrate new system into the corporate strategy. Jo and Bang (2023) tested the relationship of top management support also to continues usage of ERP and results show strong support.

As Saleh et al. (2013) suggested it is essential for upper management to give assistance and provide needed resources even in the post-implementation stages, therefore the presence of top management in all stages of an adoption is expected and mandatory. The study by Hasan et al. (2018) examined 13 internal factors,

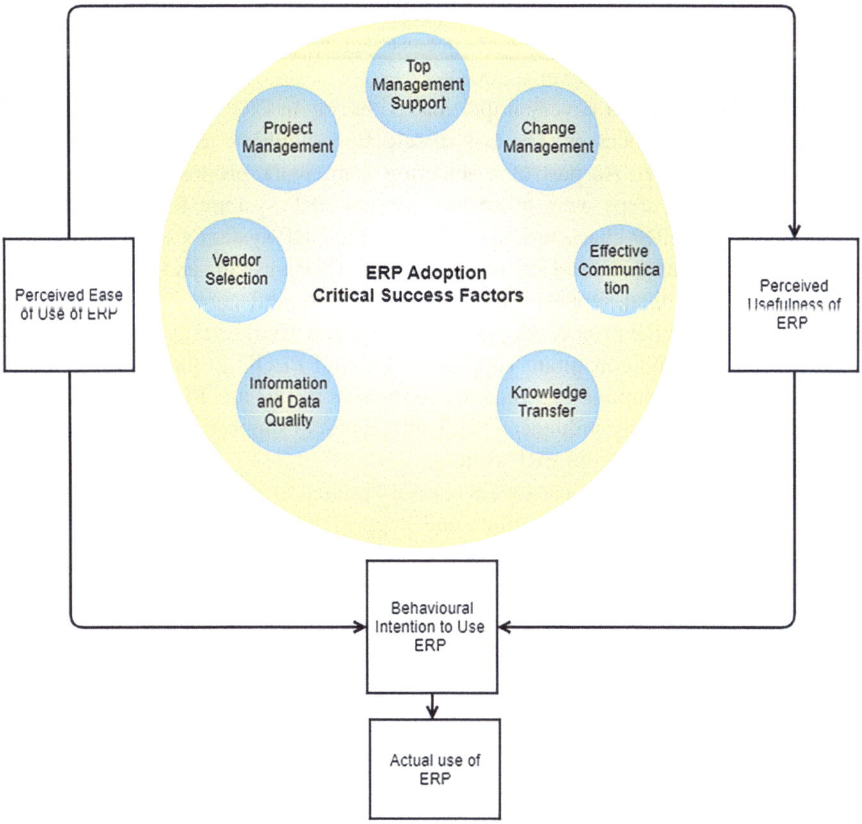

Fig. 2.4 TAM and critical success factors (Author's work)

including senior management, project management, change management, and corporate culture. According to their report, top management support is the most frequently cited critical success factor. Project management is the second most frequently mentioned critical success factor for ERP implementation.

Project Management—Creating project team, monitoring the project and meeting deadlines is the responsibility of project management. The majority of ERP projects are not successfully implemented (Ara & Al-Mudimigh, 2011). One of the main reasons for poor implementation is poor project management support (Bhatti, 2005). Most of the ERP implementations have either missed the deadline or been over the budget (Stendard & Bobek, 2013). TAM was used by Gyampah and Salam in 2004 to investigate project communications, training, and shared beliefs. The findings indicate that training and communication affect PU and PEOU's use of technology. In order to avoid increased costs and extended deadlines, companies should appoint a project management team, led by a project manager who coordinates various parts of the company and stays in close relationship with other department's managers. The members of the adoption project team should be skilled and commit full time to the project. Skills of project manager and execution team qualifications are seen as very high rated success factors (Francoise, 2009; Somers & Nelson, 2004; Dawson & Owens, 2008).

Vendor Selection—It is very important to choose an ERP system that suits and integrates business processes. The task of selecting should be assigned to a special team (Rabaa'i, 2009). As part of a selection framework proposed by Wei et al. (2005) a following steps were taken to select an ERP system: forming a project team, identifying ERP characteristics, defining the ERP system's scope and goals, filtering out unqualified vendors, evaluating the ERP system, and discussing the results. Also, technical support from the vendor side and consultant support has been tested in the ERP project adoption. Jabraoui and Touil (2022) tested the influence of technical and consultant support on PU and PEOU in the companies and found that technical support significantly influences PEOU and PU and that consultant support in positively influences PU. Both technical support and consultant support help successfully accept ERP system.

Another important factor for success closely related to vendor selection is ability to customize software functionalities and support implementation. According to Panorama Consulting (2012) 38% of companies required minor customization, 32% some customization, 12% significant, only 11% did not need customization and 9% was spread on completely and extremely customized system. Businesses need to customize their ERP system either themselves if they use open source software or with specialized vendor.

Change Management—Change management and effective communications are labeled as high level critical success factors for ERP adoption (Al-Fawaz et al., 2010). The key to smooth ERP implementations and transitions is strong change management, and end users must know what is expected of them and how to fulfill their obligations (Seo, 2013). ERP projects often fail because of inadequate user training and education (Somers & Nelson, 2001). Monk and Wagner (2013) argue that people aren't afraid of change if they know what they're doing. Getting employees familiar with all potential changes after the software is implemented is the best way to ensure a smooth implementation. Maintaining knowledge of an ERP system while using it can be challenging for end-users. Education and training are essential for the successful implementation of ERP (Meinke, 2002). ERP projects often fail because of inadequate user training and education (Somers & Nelson, 2001).

Information and Data Quality—A key component of IS implementation is information quality (DeLone & McLean, 1992), as well as ERP implementation (Xu et al., 2002). One of the main advantages of an ERP system is the consolidation of data from different departments and sources. However, if the information input into the system is incorrect or inconsistent, it can lead to inaccurate reporting, decision-making and financial results. Data collection, data validation and error correcting must be performed prior to data transfer into ERP database. It has been suggested that companies that fail to implement ERP due to centralized structures or lack of experience should seek external support (Fang et al., 2005). The success of ERP implementations is attributed to the availability of experienced and knowledgeable consultants, according to Hasibuan and Dantes (2012). Often, data import requires involvement of skilled external IT consultants. Jo and Bang (2023) combined TAM with other models and performed research for ERP intention to continue using ERP. They tested information quality and systems quality against PU and PEOU. The findings suggested that information quality positively influences PU and PEOU in the ERP adoption,

Knowledge Transfer—ERP project success is more likely if knowledge transfer is promoted. Knowledge transfer can be done from individual to individual (through communication) and through explicit sources such as ERP. ERP as a tool can transfer knowledge from one individual to another if business processes are integrated into ERP. ERP solutions offer knowledge management modules that store operating procedures and make them accessible to all users. Knowledge transfer and the types of knowledge available for ERP adoption are covered in the next chapter. Knowledge Transfer and Knowledge Communication, Management Support for Learning, Knowledge Communication and Knowledge Conversion are critical success factors for adoption (Handzic et al., 2007; Čeljo, 2022; Dasgupta & Gupta, 2009; Lin, 2007).

2.5 ERP Adoption Stages and Implementation Approaches

As literature suggests some of the major critical success factors for ERP adoption are discussed in Sect. 2.4. Practically these success factors should be taken into consideration when preparing to adopt the new ERP system or change the current version of the existing system. Figure 2.5 lists proposed ERP adoption stages for successful adoption of ERP system. Each of these stages has its own sub-stages. This section provides an overview of proposed stages and sub-stages taking into consideration critical success factors found in the literature.

In the pre-evaluation stage internal management and company executives perform a thorough analysis of the company's needs. Further, a team from different areas or departments of the company is formed that will evaluate current operations and define possible bottlenecks in the processes. This team we refer as internal ERP adoption group. The internal ERP adoption team is composed of top management representative for ERP project, managers of all departments involved in ERP project and technical or IT personnel in charge of the current IT resources. All processes are identified and together with team managers possible inconsistencies are mapped.

2.5.1 The Pre-evaluation Stage

The pre-evaluation stage is composed of three steps as shown in Fig. 2.6.

1. **Analysis of internal human resources**—The goal of this analysis is to identify who is expected to work in the ERP system and which modules of ERP are

Fig. 2.5 ERP Adoption Process (Author's work)

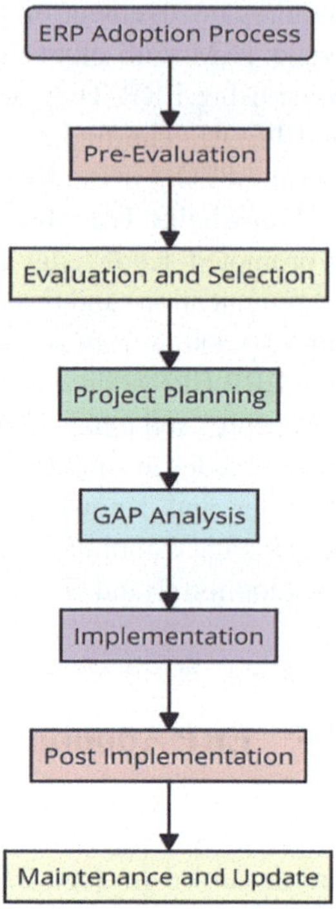

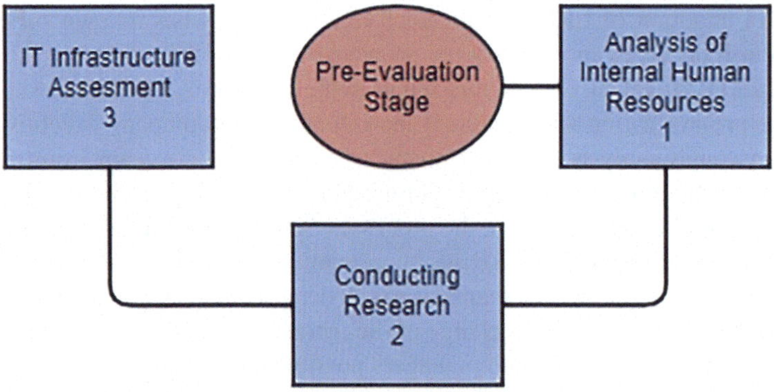

Fig. 2.6 Pre-evaluation stage (Author's work)

needed. At this stage the complete picture of expected benefits should be understood in terms of process integration and functionality improvements.

2. **Conducting research**—In this step we identify possible ERP solutions and vendors that can answer the questions about our needs and expected changes. Vendors should be able explain in details integration needs and present possible solutions to our team. We should consider on premise and cloud-based ERP

options. Our internal adoption team needs to communicate with vendors throughout the stages of ERP adoption.

3. **IT infrastructure assessment**—Complete assessment of existing IT infrastructure and possible upgrades and purchases of additional hardware and software. This step evaluates existing conditions of hardware, network components, systems software, application software, and security software. In this we define existing IT team members and analyze possible increase or decrease in team members based on the ERP system requirements.

2.5.2 Evaluation and Selection Stage

Continuing from the pre-evaluation stage, the next critical phase in ERP adoption is the evaluation and selection stage. This phase demands a focused approach to sift through potential ERP solutions and choose the one that best fits the organization's requirements. Let's break down this stage into five steps as shown in Fig. 2.7.

1. **Developing evaluation criteria**—Vendor consideration criteria reflect the business needs defined in stage 1. Business needs, IT infrastructure set-up and planned budget play the biggest role as criteria for vendor evaluation.
2. **Vendor assessment and shortlisting**—Using criteria, organizations examine ERP vendors' offerings, support services, and track records. This process leads

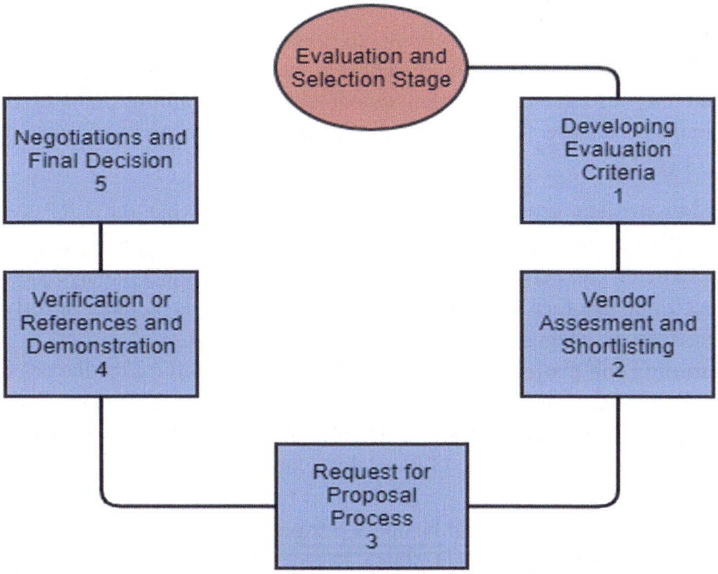

Fig. 2.7 Evaluation and selection stage (Author's work)

to the shortlisting of vendors whose systems show the potential to meet the defined needs most effectively.

3. **Request for Proposal (RFP) process**—Shortlisted vendors are asked to provide detailed information and proposals using the RFP process. Using that information, companies can compare ERP solutions based on their capabilities, costs, and implementation strategies.
4. **Verification of references and demonstrations**—Demonstrations give visitors an idea of how each ERP system works and how it works. During demonstrations members of the internal adoption group defined in stage one can see specific modules and functionalities. Getting feedback from current users provides valuable insight into how the systems perform in real-world scenarios and the quality of vendor support.
5. **Negotiations and final selection**—A careful analysis of the information gathered leads to the selection of an ERP system that meets the requirements defined by the company's adoption team. After the final selection negotiation takes place in securing favorable terms, pricing, and technical support services.

2.5.3 Project Planning Phase

Third stage of adoption process is the project planning phase for ERP implementation. It is important to create clear, actionable plans during the project planning phase of ERP implementations in order to guide the implementation process in the right direction. Project managers need to create a project plan that aligns the implementation of ERP system to the expectations identified by the internal adoption team beforehand. This plan needs to be approved by top management to meet strategic goals and operational demands. During the planning stage, the scope, objectives, timeline, resources, risk management strategies, training plans and change management procedure for the project are defined. Four steps of this stage are shown in Fig. 2.8.

1. **Defining project scope and objectives**—Defining what the ERP system is intended to do, including what it will cover and the outcomes it intends to produce, so that it can perform to the best of its abilities. Project managers define the project scope together with owners of the processes. This includes specifying the processes to be integrated, and improvements expected.
2. **Assembling the project team**—Internal adoption group makes the selection of cross-functional team responsible for project execution. This team that will be engaged in the implementation and direct communication with a vendor and consultants. It should include IT specialists, key users from various departments, department managers, and top management representative to ensure the project aligns with both technical and business perspectives.
3. **Developing a detailed project plan**—Discuss the creation of a comprehensive project plan that includes timelines, milestones, resource allocations, and

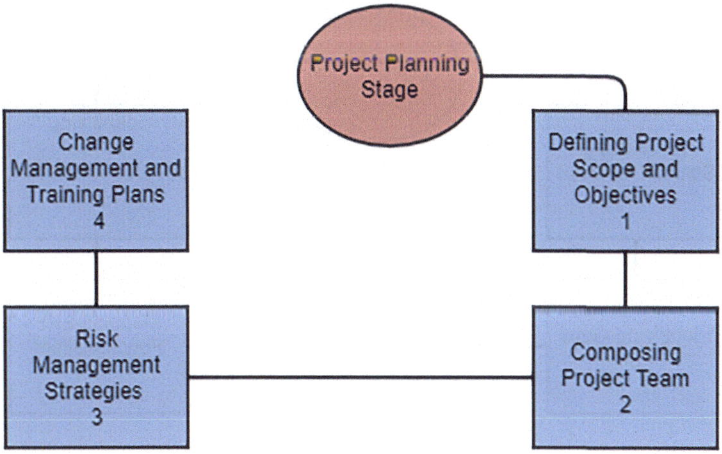

Fig. 2.8 Evaluation and ERP project management (Author's work)

budgeting. Detailed project also labels specific steps in the project with potential risk.

4. **Risk management strategies**—Identifying potential risks and developing protection strategies. The project is kept on schedule despite unforeseen challenges such as technical obstacles, budget overruns, vendor related problems, IT infrastructure supplying etc.
5. **Change management and training plans**—Managing change and establishing training ground for end users is one of the major success factors found in the theory. It involves preparing employees for changes in how they perform daily activities. Complete and detailed training plans are created and distributed to end users for smooth transition. The implementation of a new ERP system requires effective change management and comprehensive training plans.

2.5.4 Gap Analysis Stage

Transitioning from project planning, the next critical phase in the ERP adoption journey is the Gap Analysis stage. As a bridge between current business processes and the capabilities of the new ERP system, the Gap Analysis stage is crucial in ERP adoption. At this stage the system is aligned with the company's needs and objectives. Figure 2.9 provides steps needed for detailed GAP analysis.

1. **Identifying current processes and needs**—A process mapping stage begins with the collection of existing business processes. Comparing understanding of each process is needed to compare the current state with available functionalities in selected ERP. Involvement of the most knowledgeable employees in the process is required.

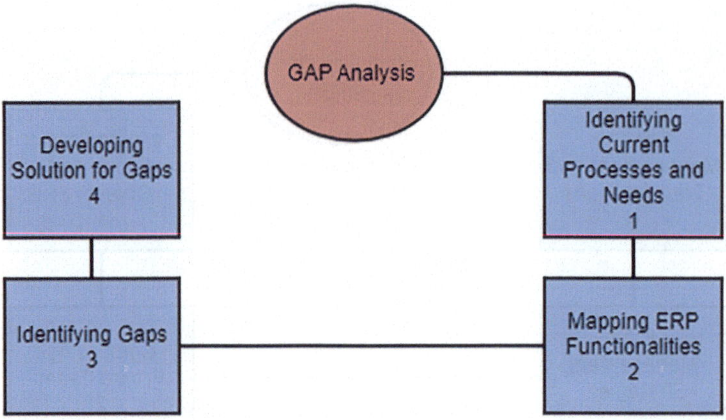

Fig. 2.9 GAP Analysis (Author's work)

2. **Mapping ERP functionalities**—Mapping is conducted between ERP system functionalities and business processes and requirements. In this step identification and recording of key operations, workflows, data flows and personnel involved is performed.
3. **Identifying gaps**—Identifying gaps between the current processes and the selected ERP functionalities is critical. The adoption team identifies the gaps and categorizes them according to potential operational impact. Gaps with higher impact on operations will be addressed first and gaps with smaller impact can be addressed over time.
4. **Developing solutions for gaps**—Each gap is addressed with a solution. The ERP software may need to be customized to meet specific business requirements or business processes may need to be reengineered according to ERP best practices. An approach is selected based on its cost-effectiveness, feasibility, and potential impact on business operations.

2.5.5 Implementation Methods and Stages

The next Implementation stage is the most action-oriented phase in the ERP adoption process, where all previous stages transfer into the action. This stage involves the actual setup, customization, and deployment of the ERP system. Besides the vendor, it also requires constant involvement of all internal adoption team members and external consultants.

Before actual implementation start, we need to be familiar with implementation approaches that are mostly used in ERP adoption process and decide which one is best suited for our company.

Big bang implementation method—Big Bang approach is when all modules of the ERP system are rolled out at once. The time limits are set by upper management of the company and systems gets used by all users from different departments at the specified time.

When switching to a new ERP system, all departments, locations, and facilities are affected. It is challenging to return to the previous system's usage after the implementation. In this approach, the implementation time is shorter, the cost is lower, all end users are trained prior to rollout, and all users start using the system on the same date. Several disadvantages are also present, such as rushing to start using the system and overlooking some details, and how unplanned failures can affect cross-functional teams. Switching to an ERP system at a given time brings additional stress for end users.

Gradual or phased approach—The second method is gradual or phased implementation, and it happens in increments. In this approach, project team members can focus on regular activities. A phased rollout of production units based on geographical location is an option for different locations with many users. In this approach, each location and individual switch to ERP according to different schedules. The phased approach requires additional standard operating procedures documents. These procedures contain a clear schedule of locations and modules used at a specific time. Also, in a phased approach, the more significant areas in the company are rolled out first. This happens when we roll out ERP based on business process priority. Advantages of phased rollout are: there is more time to adapt to the system, more time to implement lessons learned from the previous phase and choose models or functions to implement first. Some disadvantages include less urgency to complete the project, a more complicated return to the old system, and longer change time for employees. This leads to more resistance and discomfort.

Parallel approach—The third approach is the parallel approach, which uses both the old and new ERP systems simultaneously until all functions are functional. This approach is used by many companies in order to reduce the risk of failure, but it is less efficient since every input must be made in both the old and new systems. Also, this approach requires maintenance of both infrastructures which increases the cost.

Hybrid approach—The fourth approach is the hybrid rollout approach, in which phased and parallel rollout approaches are combined according to the needs of the organization. Implementing this approach has the advantage of being more controlled and less risky, but can be very costly.

The top management and adoption team will make a decision on which approach is the best to follow. These decisions are influenced by a number of factors such as: complexity of the project, number of locations, which type of business process is covered at which location, number of end users involved, and risk involved.

Upon the final decision on the method, we can start actual implementation using the steps described in Fig. 2.10.

System setup and configuration—It involves installing and configuring ERP application software to meet project needs. All systems software is installed and configured with all physical servers and databases up and running.

Data migration—During this process, data validity and integrity are ensured, information is transferred from legacy systems without loss or corruption. Valid and

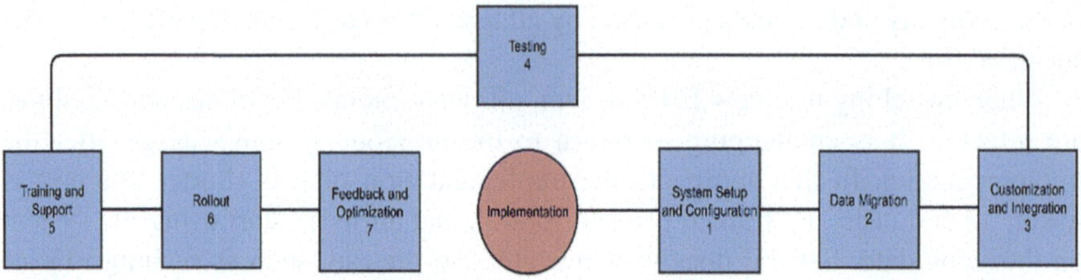

Fig. 2.10 ERP Implementation (Author's work)

clean data can also be entered for the first time if we cannot establish accuracy and integrity of present data. Primary database is established. Also, secondary database is usually brought up with replication of data from the primary database. Testing environment is prepared with the same functionality as the primary.

The customization and integration of software—Involves updating code or changing existing application configuration to add new features, and functionalities. These features are not available in the installed version of the software. In order to complete this step, the business's operational needs must be fully understood as well as the ERP capabilities.

Testing—Testing the functionality of an ERP system includes systems software testing, functionality testing, network testing (under the load), backup testing, data replication testing and user acceptance testing. The owners of the process from the adoption team need to test and approve the workflows and correct functionality of each process together with end users from their departments.

Training and support—For a smooth transition to the new system, end-users must be trained and ready to use ERP modules and features. Training documentation and instructions must be verified, approved and delivered to each end user. Communication plan in the case of the problem needs to be distributed to the end users.

Rollout—The rollout process marks the official switchover to the upgraded or new ERP system. Official switching to the new system depends on the implementation strategy we chose. Also, when defining rollout start time internal adoption team needs to coordinate with top management and financial department to define most suitable time for the switch. The system should be closely monitored to ensure any issues can be identified and resolved as soon as possible. End user input at this stage is crucial for future enhancements.

Feedback and optimization—Each owner of the process should collect feedback from end users about systems' performance in their departments and share it with adoption team. Based on possible feedback optimization is initiated either with internal IT team or vendor's consultants.

2.5.6 *Post-implementations Steps*

Post-Implementation—The Post-Implementation stage deals with continuous improvement of ERP functionality in order to bring maximum benefits to the company. Continues improvement can be based on improvement of software functionalities but also can be based on reengineering internal processes and accepting change. This phase involves continuous assessment, optimization, and alignment of the system with evolving business processes and goals. Figure 2.11 provides post-implementation stage steps.

ERP monitoring and optimization—Based on feedback and continuous monitoring of ERP performance, optimization opportunities are identified and suggested. Optimization opportunities are communicated directly to the vendor or internal IT team.

Continuous training—New training material on new functionalities, procedures and updates needs to be communicated with adoption team and end users. Trainings are planned to keep end users proficient and informed about all changes in the software. Also, trainings improve the overall user satisfaction.

Change management—Effective support of all employees included in using ERP. If present additional gaps in the processes are identified and communicated with vendor. Changes in roles and jobs are also identified and communicated with owners of the process.

Operations strategy alignment—Improvements of ERP software performed through optimization or additional functionality development are checked to match and satisfy operational strategic decisions and workflows.

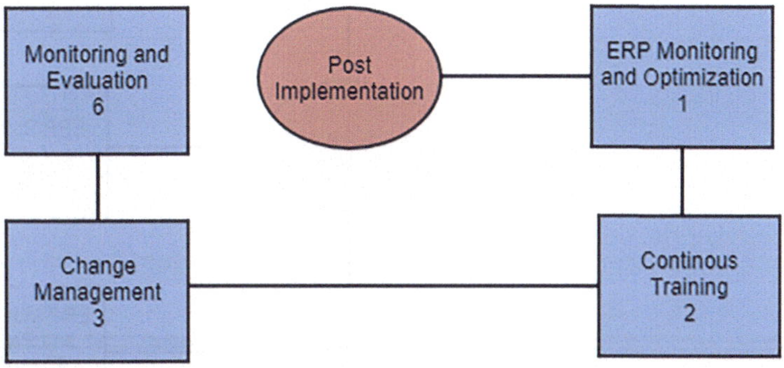

Fig. 2.11 ERP post-implementation (Author's work)

2.5.7 Maintenance and Update Stage

The final stage of ERP adoption process is continuous system maintenance and update. In this stage we are continuously keeping our ERP system up-to-date, safe and efficient. Three steps shown in Fig. 2.12 define this last stage:

ERP software updates—Regular upgrades of functionality and security keep data safe and reliable. High security measures need to be implemented by the IT team to make the system less vulnerable. It is recommended that ERP updates are in line with the latest vendor's software version available. Staying current with the latest version improves functionality and security.

ERP Software Audit—Depending on the industry where ERP software is used, software audits and standardization can be required. Aligning ERP procedures with industry management standards (ex: ISO 9001 and ISO 27001) is an advantage for the organization or company.

ERP monitoring and process evaluation—Ongoing monitoring and periodic audit of the ERP system's performance is recommended in order to identify areas for improvement. Monitoring software can be used to identify and acknowledge delays in the process or glitches in the system. System should be improved continuously in order to support and improve operations and follow up with strategic business decisions.

2.6 System Adoption Responsibilities and Documentation

After we have analysed all stages of ERP adoption we need to describe how the responsibilities flow between parties involved and what types of documents are following each stage.

Fig. 2.12 ERP maintenance and update (Author's work)

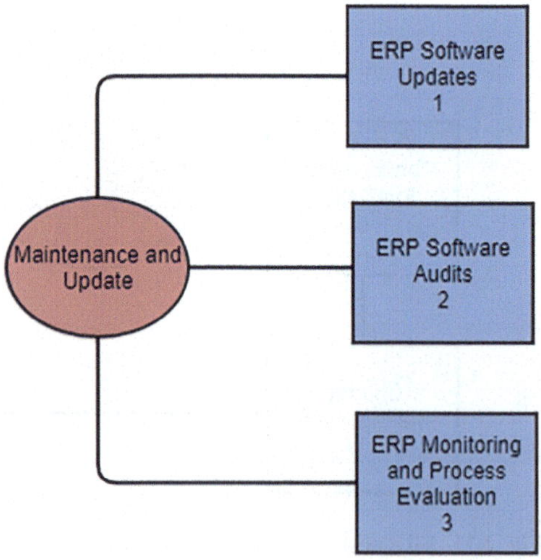

In the Pre-Evaluation stage top management of the company initiates the need for the ERP system. In order to further analyse real needs of the company, find current state of business processes and perform research of possible ERP vendors, internal adoption team is created. Internal adoption team consists of top management representative, most knowledgeable employees from each process, IT personnel and project manager. This team performs analysis of present employees and positions, understand what kind of applications and solutions are needed and what is the current state of IT infrastructure. Based on these information research about possible ERP vendors is conducted and first contacts is established.

In the Evaluation and Selection stage internal adoption created criteria for vendor evaluation. Team evaluates the references of possible ERP vendors. Based on criteria matching and references team creates Request for Proposal (RFP) for final group of selected vendors. In this stage final selection of ERP vendor is made according to best fit for company's operational needs. The project is officially announced and we can start with detailed project planning.

In the Project Planning stage internal adoption team with ERP vendor defines scopes, objectives and responsibilities and creates detailed project plan. Project plan includes budget planned for the each stage of the project. Budget also includes the spending for external consultants that will be engaged in the project. Risk management plan identifies possible risks in the project and provides actions that need to be taken to keep the project running on time. Change management plan are also created in this stage to prepare end users and other employees for implementation. Also, this plan includes effective communication with end users, training materials, possible incentive plan and internal promotion plan for active and engaged end users.

In the Gap Analysis stage internal adoption team and particularly process owners or most knowledgeable employees from departments create Business Process Requirements and test functional requirements with available functionalities in the ERP modules. The testing stage is performed together with ERP vendor team and external consultants. In this process mapping charts and reports for each individual process is created and possible gaps are identified. It department identifies all system requirements needed for rollout of new system. This report includes all hardware, software and networking resources needed. Based on the gap analysis report ERP vendor performs customization of needed functionalities and new customized solution are presented to internal adoption team and tested.

After all testing has received positive feedback from internal adoption team we start with implementation process. All parties are heavily involved. Internal adoption team, vendor team and external consultants create and distribute detailed training manuals for each end user based on its own job description. Trainings are performed by ERP vendor team and external consultants. Internal adoption team together with its end users are taking training sessions. After the internal adoption team acknowledges that data is error free and clean the vendor starts with data migration. Final testing is performed on the testing platform created by the vendor. The final rollout checklist of all human resources and IT resources ready for rollout is created. The rollout takes place in defined time by top management and internal adoption team. Our rollout schedule will depend on the method of the implementation we chose. After the rollout has taken place internal adoption are collecting all inputs from end users and project manager communicates with vendor about this feedback.

Post-Implementation stage involves continuous monitoring of ERP functionalities. Thru monitoring possible additional customization is defined and communicated with vendor. After rollout changes in daily activities are recorded and communicated with department managers. Vendor delivers improved functionalities and monitors the overall health of the platform thru system log, user report and application logs. Additional training where needed is initiated to the vendor.

In the final Maintenance and Update stage IT department follows the procedure of regular communication with vendor and performs regular updates of application, system and security software. Also, it is recommended to perform software audits and align ERP functionalities with industry management standards as much as possible. Monitoring and continuous feedback from end users and departments is recommended. Figure 2.13 presents all responsibilities and documents required in the ERP adoption process.

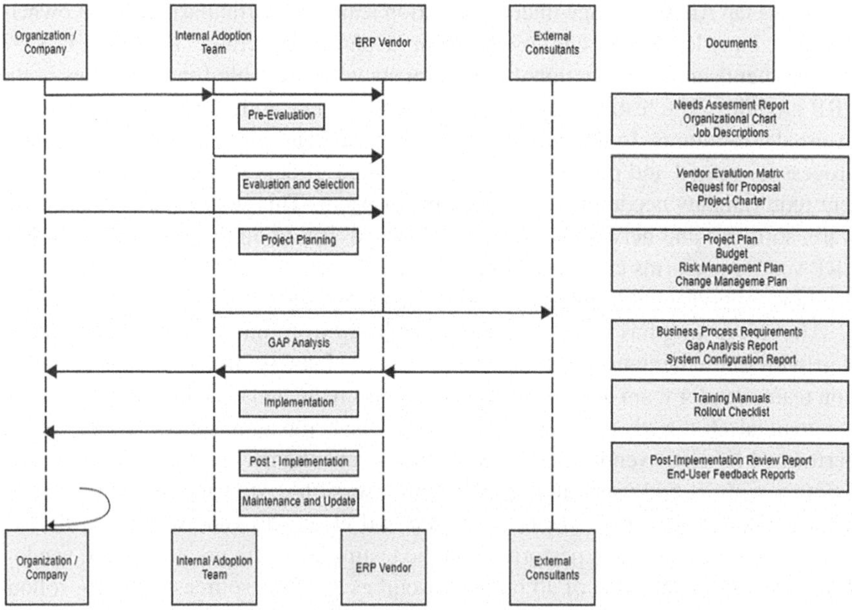

Fig. 2.13 Adoption responsibilities matrix and documents flow (Author's work)

2.7 Conclusions

The adoption process takes in consideration organizational, technical and process activities. ERP adoption process is of the greatest importance for companies or organizations implementing the new or changing existing ERP solution. Researchers in the IS field use different models and theories that study adoption, acceptance and implementation for and ERP systems. Mostly used and well accepted model, Technology Acceptance Model is discussed as well as prior findings of the usage of this model in ERP adoption. Major critical factors studied in the chapter are: top management, project management, change management, information and data quality, knowledge transfer and vendor selection. These critical success factors are further used to present practical adoption models with its stages and sub-activities. Companies need to choose corresponding implementation methods as a part of adoption process. The chapter concludes with explanation of responsibilities, roles and documents that follow each step described in the model. This chapter can be used both by the teaching community and practitioners in the field of Information systems and management.

References

Al-Fawaz, K., Eldabi, T., & Naseer, A. (2010). *Challenges and influential factors in ERP adoption and implementation.*

Ara, A., & Al-Mudimigh, A. S. (2011). The role and impact of project management in ERP project implementation life cycle. *Global Journal of Computer Science and Technology, 11*(5), 7–10.

Bhatti, T. (2005). Critical success factors for the implementation of enterprise resource planning (ERP): Empirical validation. *The second international conference on innovation in information technology (IIT'05)* (pp. 1–10). College of Business, Zayed University.

Čeljo, A. (2022). *Technology acceptance model (TAM) based approach to adoption and use of integrated business information systems*, PhD thesis, University of Srajevo, School of Economics and Business in Sarajevo.

Chuttur, M. (2009). *Overview of the technology acceptance model: Origins, developments and future directions.* Retrieved November 30, 2014, from sprouts: Working papers on information systems: http://sprouts.aisnet.org/785/1/TAMReview.pdf

Dasgupta, M., & Gupta, R. (2009). Innovation in organizations: A review of the role of organizational learning and knowledge management. *Global Business Review, 10*(2), 203–224.

Davis, F. D. (1985). *A technology acceptance model for empirically testing new end-user information systems: Theory and results* (Doctoral dissertation, Massachusetts Institute of Technology).

Davis, F. D., Bagozzi, R. P., & Warshaw, P. R. (1989). User acceptance of computer technology: A comparison of two theoretical models. *Management Science, 35*(8), 982–1003.

Dawson, J., & Owens, J. (2008). Critical success factors in the chartering phase: A case study of an ERP implementation. *International Journal of Enterprise Information Systems (IJEIS), 4*(3), 9–24.

DeLone, W., & McLean., E. (1992). Information systems success: The quest for the dependent variable. *Information Systems Research, 3*(1), 60–95.

Dillon, A., & Morris, M. G. (1996). User acceptance of new information technology: Theories and models. *Review of Information Science and Technology, 14*(4), 3–32.

Fang, L., Patrecia, S., & Seigerroth, U. (2005). *Critical success factors in ERP implementation*. Jönköping International Business School.

Francoise, O. (2009). ERP implementation through critical success factors management. *Business Process Management Journal, 15*(3), 371–393.

Hancerliogullari Koksalmis, G., & Damar, S. (2022). An empirical evaluation of a modified technology acceptance model for SAP ERP system. *Engineering Management Journal, 34*(2), 201–216.

Handzic, M., Lagumdzija, A., & Celjo, A. (2007). A survey of knowledge management adoption in public administration. *Journal of Information & Knowledge Management, 6*(3), 219–230.

Hasan, M., Ebrahim, Z., Mahmood, W., & Ra. (2018). Factors influencing Enterprise resource planning system: A review. *Journal of Advanced Manufacturing Technology (JAMT), 12*(1), 247–258.

Hasibuan, Z. A., & Dantes, G. R. (2012). Priority of key success factors (KSFS) on enterprise resource planning (ERP) system implementation life cycle. *Journal of Enterprise Resource Planning Studies, 2012*, 1–15.

Ibrahimović, S., & Bajgoric, N. (2018). The role of information system monitoring in improving system availability. In *In always-on enterprise information systems for modern organizations* (pp. 184–207). IGI-Global.

Jabraoui, S., & Touil, A. A. (2022). Managing implementation of the ERP systems: The importance of technical and consultant support. *Marketing i menedžment innovacij, 13*(4), 173–183.

Jo, H., & Bang, Y. (2023). Understanding continuance intention of enterprise resource planning (ERP): TOE, TAM, and IS success model. *Heliyon, 9*(10), e21019.

Lee, J., Siau, K., & Hong, S. (2003). Enterprise integration with ERP and EAI communications of the ACM. *Communications of the ACM, 46*, 54–60.

Leyh, C. (2016). *Critical success factors for ERP projects in small and medium-sized enterprises—The perspective of selected ERP system vendors*. Springer International Publishing Switzerland.

Lin, H. (2007). Knowledge sharing and firm innovation capability: An empirical study. *International Journal of Manpower, 28*(3/4), 315–332.

Loh, T. C., & Koh*, S. C. L. (2004). Critical elements for a successful enterprise resource planning implementation in small-and medium-sized enterprises. *International Journal of Production Research, 42*(17), 3433–3455.

Meinke, J. (2002). *Training: Key to effective enterprise resource planning implementation*. University of Maryland.

Monk, E., & Wagner, B. (2013). *Concepts in enterprise resource planning*. Course Technology.

Nah, F. F. H., & Delgado, S. (2006). Critical success factors for enterprise resource planning implementation and upgrade. *Journal of Computer Information Systems, 46*(5), 99–113.

Panorama Consulting. (2012). *Lessons learned from a government ERP failure*. Retrieved from Panorama Consulting: http://www.immagic.com/eLibrary/ARCHIVES/GENERAL/PANCONUS/P121121L.pdf

Rabaa'i, A. (2009). Identifying critical success factors of ERP Systems at the Higher Education Sector. In *Third international symposium on innovation in Information & Communication Technology*. Queensland University of Technology (QUT).

Saleh, M., Abbad, M., & Al-Shehri, M. (2013). ERP implementation success factors in Saudi Arabia. *International Journal of Computer Science and Security*, 15–30.

Seo, G. (2013, 5). *Challenges in implementing enterprise resource planning (ERP) system in large organizations: Similarities and differences between corporate and university environment*. Retrieved from http://ic3.mit.edu/ResearchSamples/2013-07.pdf

Somers, T., & Nelson, K. (2001). The impact of critical success factors across the stages of Enterprise resource planning implementations. In *34th annual Hawaii international conference on system sciences* (HICSS-34), 8, p. 8016.

Somers, T., & Nelson, K. (2004). A taxonomy of players and activities across the ERP project life cycle. *Information & Management, 41*(3), 257–278.

Sternad, S., & Bobek, S. (2013). Impacts of TAM-based external factors on ERP acceptance. *Procedia Technology, 9*, 33–42.

Umble, E., Haft, R., & Umble, M. (2003). Enterprise resource planning: Implementation procedures and critical success factors. *European Journal of Operational Research, 146*(2), 241–257.

Venkatesh, V., & Bala, H. (2008). Technology acceptance model 3 and a research agenda on interventions. *Decision Sciences, 39*(2), 273–315.

Venkatesh, V., & Davis, F. D. (1996). A model of the antecedents of perceived ease of use: Development and test. *Decision Sciences, 27*(3), 451–481.

Venkatesh, V., & Davis, F. D. (2000). A theoretical extension of the technology acceptance model: Four longitudinal field studies. *Management Sciences, 46*(2), 186–204.

Verma, S., & Kumar, A. (2013). Critical success factors for ERP implementation towards. *International Journal of Advanced Research in Computer Science and Software Engineering*, 141–144.

Wei, C., Chien, C., & Wang, M. (2005). An AHP-based approach to ERP system selection. *International Journal of Production Economics, 96*(1), 47–62.

Xu, H., Horn Nord, J., Brown, N., & Daryl Nord, G. (2002). Data quality issues in implementing an ERP. *Industrial Management & Data Systems, 102*(1), 47–58.

Yayla, A., & Hu, Q. (2007). User acceptance of e-commerce technology: A meta-analytic comparison of competing models. *13th European conference on information systems (ECIS 2007)*. Retrieved from http://works.bepress.com/qing_hu/48

Chapter 3
ERP and Knowledge Management

3.1 Introduction

KM and ERP systems work together as a bridge linking information systems with cognitive assets of the company. These two initiatives, ERP and KM, have been and are getting implemented by many companies (Davenport et al., 1998). Data generated by daily operations is stored in the ERP systems database. When this data is transformed into meaningful information and actionable knowledge the company is able to use it for innovation. This is where KM processes step in—they are designed to ensure that information is not only stored but also appropriately managed. KM focuses on the flow of knowledge and makes it accessible and useful throughout the company.

Interaction of ERP and KM offers several tangible benefits. Combining ERP and KM systems provides employees with comprehensive data and contextual knowledge, supporting better decision-making. This integration ensures that executive management can use output from ERP that is based not only on data but also with experiential knowledge from the process operations. Access to a consolidated pool of knowledge and data improves creativity and innovation. Employees can leverage historical data and collective expertise stored in KM systems to develop new solutions and improve existing processes. Integrating KM with ERP modules helps in capturing knowledge from employee's experiences that can be lost when they leave. This makes valuable information readily available to other team members, ensuring continuity and supporting company's learning. Also, integration of ERP and KM improves the collaboration between departments. Uniform platform that contains valuable and up to date information which can be shared and used by different departments cuts down silos effect and improves efficiency. Companies that maintain separate platforms for ERP and KMS can cost benefit by integrating these two platforms.

L. Turulja et al., *Integrating ERP Systems and Knowledge Management*, Progress in IS, https://doi.org/10.1007/978-3-031-68922-2_3

On the other hand, there are disadvantages that we have to take in consideration before integrating ERP and KM. Initial cost for integration of ERP and KMS can be very high. Besides both systems costs can be increased if integration involves hardware and infrastructure upgrades and customization. The complex implementation of both systems can be time-consuming. Implementation requires careful planning in order to ensure data compatibility and cut down the possibility of disruption of daily operations. As discussed in ERP adoption chapter adoption by employees is crucial. They might resist adoption due to discomfort of learning new interfaces and procedures. Post integration, ongoing costs for platform maintenance and data security measures implementation can also be high. Also, relying heavily on an integrated ERP and KM system can make a company vulnerable to system failures or data loss. Such dependencies may critically impact operations if the system experiences downtime or other technical issues. These disadvantages highlight the need for careful consideration and strategic planning before deciding to integrate ERP and KM systems, ensuring that the benefits outweigh the potential drawbacks.

The interaction between ERP systems and Knowledge Management is process with the potential to transform the operational dynamics of the company. In this chapter we continue to analyze adoption factors from the KM perspective for successful ERP adoption. Further, we provide an overview of knowledge types and knowledge creation process. Knowledge transfer/sharing, and knowledge quality are considered as major success factors for ERP adoption. In the last part of the chapter, we focus on knowledge transfer approaches and knowledge management during ERP adoption process. ERP adoption process phases and KM cycles are used to identify knowledge transfer types and knowledge dimensions according to SECI model.

3.2 Knowledge Types

According to Nonaka et al. (1996) and Polanyi (1966), knowledge can be classified into knowledge types and structures. This knowledge can be classified into two categories: explicit and tacit.

Explicit knowledge is usually found in rules and working procedures. It is stored in databases, notes and documents. Explicit knowledge can be easily transferred without requiring person-to-person contact. It can be used by different media and formats, allowing it to reach a wide audience efficiently. It is a kind of knowledge that can be easily managed by knowledge management systems (KMS) which is extremely efficient in supporting paper and script storage, retrieval, and sharing.

Word "tacit" means to perform the activities without the use of words or speech (Oxford American Dictionary, 2001). Polanyi (1966) mentions that we can know more then we can speak about. Knowledge that is usually not openly expressed is referred as tacit knowledge (Wagner & Sternberg, 1985). Tacit knowledge is set up in the human minds, it includes cultural beliefs and values as well as skills, capabilities and expertise. It can be challenging to verbalize and pass on tacit knowledge.

Tacit knowledge can be obtained by observation and imitation. This means that tacit knowledge can be routine based on experience and as that, it is the most appreciated source of knowledge and expertise, as well as the most probable to indicate the advances in the company.

Unlike tacit knowledge, which is held individually, or explicit knowledge, which is easily articulated and shared, embedded knowledge resides within the structures and operations of an organization or society. Embedded knowledge that is a part of specific practices, product, culture or procedures (Gamble & Blackwell, 2001). An embedded knowledge is one where knowledge is actually embedded into the product itself (operating system, application procedure, etc.). Good examples of embedded knowledge would be software coding of ERP modules. Long terms programmers that participated in the coding of these modules would be more efficient in code optimization and updates. Types of knowledge are explained in the Table 3.1.

3.3 Knowledge Creation

Knowledge creation cycle is a process that starts with raw data and ends with actionable knowledge that can be used for overall improvement in business operations and decision making. Identifying the knowledge requires an analysis of its creation process. This is the process which involves making or taking available raw data for a number of sources or processes and then creating useful information. Further interpretation and ability to understand the structured information would create

Table 3.1 Types of knowledge (Author's work)

Type of Knowledge	Main characteristics	Example
Explicit	Verbalized and documented. Transferred without person-to-person contact. Includes formal structure such as codified procedures, data and scientific formulas. Easily accessible and duplicated	Published academic research Software program user manual
Tacit	Non-verbalized. Acquired through experience. Skills acquired over time by practical performance. Transferred through mentoring or shared experiences. Not easily accessible or duplicated	Judgment made by experienced engineers about hardware and software needed based on the company size. Doctor's judgment for medical diagnosis through the based on the observations of the patient
Embedded	Built in processed or products. Acquired through long term practical involvement. Not easily transferable and updatable	Unique way of assembling the product. Smart phone embedded knowledge about user interface design or communications protocols is not available to the users but very critical for product functioning

knowledge for the company or organization. Figure 3.1 summarizes knowledge creation flow.

Knowledge creation starts with raw data collection. Raw data means unprocessed and unorganized information. It refers to the initial set of data without any meaningful interpretation or analysis. Raw data can be numerical, textual, or visual in nature, and it often requires processing to become meaningful. This type of data is captured and recorded. For example, imagine a company that sells products online. Each time the product is sold, raw data is captured and stored. The raw data could look like the example in Table 3.2.

Raw data captured in these transactions:

Order ID—transaction identifier, Customer ID—customer identification, Date—purchase date, Product ID—identifier of the item that has been sold, Time—time of transaction, Price—price that item has been sold for and Payment Method—the way that customer has paid for its purchase.

This data is raw because it's collected directly from transactions without any modification or processing. It only provides basic details for each transaction.

Information, on the other hand, refers to data that has been organized and structured into a meaningful and useful context. It is a result of transforming raw data into a format that allows for analysis and interpretation. Information may include facts, figures, statistics, and narratives that present relevant information.

In order to structure the data in the meaningful way, first we need to clean the data and make sure that there are no duplicates or errors. The second step is to organize the data for further analysis and according to relevance. This includes sorting, filtering, grouping according to 'Category' or 'Customer ID'. Third step is to be able to get general sense of data and being able to represent the results in the meaningful way. For example, performing simple statistics to getting the average of the sales of the certain item and represent it using pie chart for that certain category. Further we can continue with using correlations analysis between sales volume and price to check if lower level items sell more. We can also track the repeat rate of the certain customer to check how often this customer makes a purchase and when. Finally we can create reports based on the findings such as monthly sales reports or customer behavior selling report.

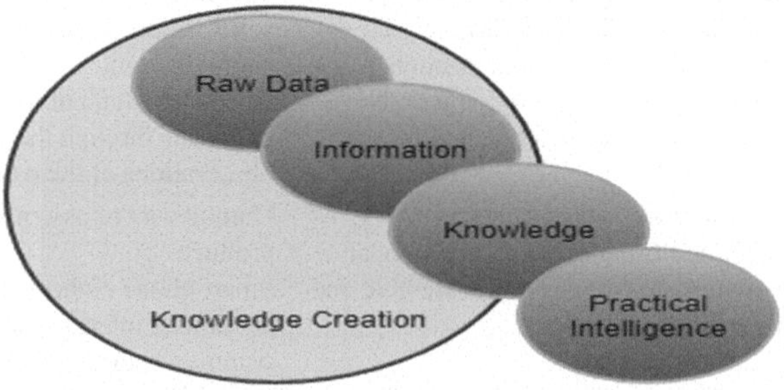

Fig. 3.1 Knowledge creation (Author's work)

Table 3.2 Data storage example (Author's work)

Order ID	Customer ID	Date	Product ID	Time	Category	Price	Payment method
001	0001	9-5-2024	0345	14:32	T-Shirt	$10	Credit Card
002	0002	9-5-2024	0457	14:56	Sweater	$32	PayPal
003	0003	9-5-2024	1357	15:03	Skirt	$55	Debit Card
004	0004	9-5-2024	0829	15:10	Hat	$28	Credit Card

Knowledge is a deeper level of understanding the information. It goes beyond facts and represents acquired experience. Knowledge is subjective and context-dependent, and it is acquired through learning, education, and experience. It is built on a foundation of information and can be acquired and applied in various domains. It is possible to define knowledge in many different ways. For Alavi and Leidner (1999), knowledge is described as information that someone holds in mind, whereas knowledge is also viewed as the result of the interaction between cognition and reality. According to Magnier-Watanabe and Benton in general, knowledge is defined as information that has been proven true or useful through experience, and is crucial for organizations to make quality decisions. In our example we could look at the structured information and try to relate data driven findings with business strategy, market conditions and customer behavior. From the data driven findings we can see what the bestselling item is, when is it sold, what is the payment method etc. Based on selling time, type of product, and pricing we can start to perform customer segmentation, generate product performance analysis or revise and improve pricing strategy. In this way we are using structured information to create actionable knowledge for the company. Also based on the sales, customer, timing, type of the product and payment method preferences information we can create knowledge for organization by building supply chain strategies, marketing campaigns and customer retention strategies. Using the knowledge inside the company separates business success from failure.

Practical intelligence, by definition it is the ability to acquire tacit knowledge from every day experience and use it in projects solving where amount of information to solve the problem is not sufficient (Cianciolo et al., 2006). It consists of the ability to apply knowledge, predict problems, and make intelligent decisions. Intelligence is not solely based on the accumulation of information but on the ability to think critically, analyze situations, and make informed decisions. It is the ability to reason, plan, and adapt to new and challenging situations. In order to achieve practical intelligence, a person must have a broad range of skills and tacit knowledge to manage others, and its career effectively (Wagner & Sternberg, 1985). As a company creates knowledge, it can move on to developing intelligence, which involves applying advanced analytical tools, machine learning models, and predictive analytics to improve decision-making. Using our example of selling company we can use predictive models to forecast future sales trends. We can also use machine learning algorithms to identify peak selling periods, anticipate product demand or identify potential selling items shortages.

Table 3.3 provides an overview and key characteristics of raw data, information, knowledge and practical intelligence.

In summary, raw data is unprocessed information, information is organized and structured data, knowledge is a deeper level of understanding of information, and intelligence is the ability to apply knowledge, solve problems, and make intelligent decisions.

3.4 Knowledge Management Critical Success Factors and ERP Adoption

Knowledge has replaced capital, land, and labour as the primary economic resources (Hwang, 2008). KM processes used to acquire knowledge and apply it in order to improve products and processes (Turulja & Bajgorić, 2018). Using and developing the knowledge assets of an organization to achieve organizational goals is the aim of knowledge management (Davenport et al., 1998). According to Burk (1999), knowledge management enables us to access and use appropriate information at the right time to make good decisions. Knowledge management also enables employees to communicate and share knowledge within an organization. In addition, it strives to ensure an organization can learn. It also ensures that it can reuse its knowledge assets in its process activities. The full extent of knowledge management is something that is not generally accepted. However, there are some remarkable differences in the definitions of knowledge management. Knowledge management refers to the whole idea of providing the right information to the right person at the right time. Our focus is on managing knowledge in ERP adoption process.

Table 3.3 Knowledge creation characteristics (Author's work)

	Raw Data	Information	Knowledge	Practical Intelligence
Definition	Unprocessed, unorganized facts collected from observations	Data that has been organized or processed to have meaning	Interpreted information, integrated with existing understanding	The ability to apply knowledge and skills in real-world situations
Characteristics	Disorganized and without context	Structured, contextual, and easier to analyze	Useful, contextual and often theoretical	With specific context and action-oriented
Form	Numbers, symbols, raw text	Structured Charts, graphs, reports, lists	Concepts, ideas, theories	Decisions, strategies, effective actions
Dependency	Foundation of all subsequent stages	Depends on raw data	Relies on information	Relies on knowledge and experience

3.4.1 Effects of KM and KMS on ERP Adoption

Members of the company will appreciate the ERP system when their minds integrate with the system (Lee & Lee, 2000) which is the most challenging task (Jones, 2005). Today, business relies on physical and knowledge assets. Companies are in need to perform their business with the help of KM. Creating, storing, using and updating the knowledge through all ERP adoption phases should be priority for adoption team and executive management. Davenport (1998) points that managing knowledge is a critical success factor in order to retain the control of operations and not be controlled by the system itself. Many companies have implemented ERP to integrate and control different business areas such as order management, purchasing, supply, and logistics (Gunasekaran et al., 2007). There is a high concern that companies will not be able to manage and maintain their ERP if they do not capture and control the ERP wide knowledge. Companies lack a clear KM vision of ERP KM practice, and need to develop structures and processes to capture and share codified and tacit knowledge (Parry & Graves, 2008). Successful ERP implementation relies on well-established adoption team and management support. A successful ERP adoption also requires knowledge sharing among team members, end users' knowledge of modules they are to use, and integration of the company's internal knowledge with the knowledge of consultants and vendors involved in the ERP adoption process (Mahendrawathi, 2015). As suggested by Markus and Tanis (2000) KM of ERP systems is one of the crucial concerns for many companies.

Knowledge management in the ERP adoption process can be seen as a process of transferring and sharing both explicit and tacit knowledge. According to Mahendrawathi (2015), organizational knowledge creation is a process that involves the conversion between tacit and explicit knowledge, such as combination, socialization, and capture. Mentorship and transfer of knowledge about processes and ERP modules usage is expected from experienced employees and consultants. ERP integrates business processes while KMS manages explicit and tacit knowledge for the use in ERP adoption process (Xu et al., 2006). All reports, documents, software models training materials can be stored in KMS. Both systems ERP and KMS are having the common goal of improving the business processes and improve operations. Experienced employees and process leaders should be a part of adoption team. Basically, there is no integration of ERP and KMS nor KM in ERP adoption without considering human factors. Employees of the organization are the ones that are main participants in knowledge creation, sharing and usage.

3.4.2 Knowledge Transfer

Knowledge sharing is also known as knowledge transfer (Huber, 2001). Sharing knowledge among employees is essential to build trust and improve teamwork. ERP implementation includes team members from different functional areas, and they need to understand and share knowledge on how they perform their daily routines. Adoption of ERP is more likely to lead to successful outcomes if an organization promotes collaboration and teamwork (Stanciu & Tinca, 2013). In order to share and transfer knowledge, there are many methods and strategies to consider. According to Nonaka and Takeuchi (2001) and Nonaka et al. (1996) and their SECI conceptual model there are four modes when it comes to knowledge transfer approach: combination, externalization internalization and socialization. Combination involves converting explicit knowledge into explicit, while socialization involves sharing tacit knowledge through interaction and experience. Internalization involves learning from external parties and converting explicit into tacit, and externalization involves translating tacit knowledge into explicit. Table 3.4 summarizes common examples of knowledge transfer approaches expected in ERP adoption process.

Knowledge transfer has been tested for ERP usage and has been found that it positively influences the use of ERP. According to Chou et al. (2014) knowledge sharing was highlighted as a critical component of ERP implementation success and its impact on ERP system usage was further confirmed. Karim et al. (2023) studied how KM factors impact ERP implementation and found that knowledge creation and knowledge sharing behavior have significant effect. When employees are happy about shared knowledge and feel satisfied, they will be willing to use the system. Proper knowledge transfer helps end users understand how the ERP system works and how they can benefit from a system. Training sessions lead to higher ERP user adoption rates. Knowledge transfer also helps overcome the user resistance and lowers the fear of using the ERP by end users. Understanding why changes are being made and how can improve their career reducing fear and resistance among employees. As users become more knowledgeable about the ERP system, they can provide valuable feedback to IT departments and system administrators about potential improvements or necessary adjustments. These comments, suggestions and ideas can be shared in the post-implementation stage with vendors to optimize the ERP functionality. The ongoing loop of feedback and suggestions leads to

Table 3.4 Knowledge transfer approach (Author's work)

Approach	Characteristic	Methods
Tacit to Tacit	Involves sharing tacit knowledge through social interactions, without formal documentation	Mentorship, informal conversations, and on-the-job training
Tacit to Explicit	Transforms tacit knowledge into explicit documents and guides that can be easily shared	Writing manuals, creating training videos and tutorials
Explicit to Explicit	Combining various pieces of explicit knowledge to create new documents or databases	Compiling reports, developing databases, and utilizing information systems
Explicit to Tacit	Occurs when individuals absorb and convert explicit knowledge into tacit knowledge	Learning by reading or doing, and through simulations and training programs

continuous improvement of the system's functionality and its alignment with organizational needs. Also, it positively influences the ERP project management as one of the crucial success factors in ERP adoption.

Information systems and digital applications improve KM because they facilitate sharing of information and knowledge (Turulja & Bajgorić, 2018). Learning can be stored through the purchase and use of KMS. KMS needs to be integrated into the corporate process flows and part of a central organizational system. Digital platforms, such as intranets, and collaborative tools can be used in order to facilitate the sharing and transfer of knowledge both within and across organizations. Structured approaches to sharing and transferring knowledge contribute to organizational growth and success while improving personal and professional development.

3.4.3 *Information Quality*

Before implementing ERP, it is imperative to establish clear goals, objectives, scope, planning, and scheduling. One of the key factors in establishing an information system and in adopting an ERP system is information quality (DeLone & McLean, 1992; Xu et al., 2006). Also, the quality of information provided by ERP or KMS is a critical factor for knowledge creation in the company. An accurate, precise, and complete information system's output is referred to as information quality (DeLone & McLean, 1992; Kuo & Lee, 2009), in the process of knowledge creation, information quality influences accuracy, reliability, and usefulness of the knowledge created.

During the evaluation and selection step information on system's quality is very important for final selection. System's quality deals with system's ability to process data and provide structured information. According to Wu and Wang (2006), system quality reflects the information system's processing capabilities and operational characteristics. Users' interactions with the system are defined by the system's quality characteristics (Zhou et al., 2010). People, organizations, and technology all play a role in determining the quality of an ERP system (Fan & Fang, 2006). By prioritizing high-quality information during ERP adoption companies and individuals can improve their analytical capabilities and decision making.

The importance of information quality in adoption of IS has been acknowledged through studies using TAM. It has been shown that perceived usefulness and perceived ease of use of different information systems are positively influenced by information quality. Kuo and Lee (2009) found that IQ significantly impacts PEU. In their study of the tax system's acceptance, Chang et al. (2005) also found that IQ is significantly related to PEU and PU. IQ is a significant determinant of PEU and PU when adopting business systems.

3.5 Knowledge Creation Through ERP

Enterprise Resource Planning (ERP) systems collect, process and store large amounts of raw data from various processes within the business. Raw data refers to unprocessed facts and figures collected directly from business activities. This data can include transaction details, customer interactions, inventory counts, and employee records. Each ERP module processes raw data according to its functional requirements. For example, the finance module calculates financial ratios from sales and expense data. In addition, the HR module analyzes employee performance data to generate appraisal reports. The transformation from raw data to structured information involves sorting, analyzing, and formatting data to make it useful for decision-making and operational management. Table 3.5, provides an explanation of how raw data is used by basic ERP modules in order to process it and create structured information.

When ERP processes captured data in order to create structured information the. The next step is the creation of knowledge. Knowledge is derived by interpreting structured information and applying it to make decisions, solve problems, or improve processes. Structured information from ERP modules can be used to create knowledge, and whether this knowledge is shown in Table 3.6.

Through the analysis of financial reports, the financial managers and executives can look at the derived information about when to invest in new assets or new resources. This leads to explicit knowledge about resource allocation and engagement. Performance reviews and employee data are further used to develop better training programs and retention strategies, which often involve tacit knowledge about organizational culture and employee needs. Information on material usage and work orders can lead to the development of new manufacturing sub processes and techniques, which are often tacit due to the hands-on, experiential nature of the knowledge. Analysis of sales trends and revenue data helps in understanding market

Table 3.5 ERP knowledge creation I (Author's work)

ERP module	Raw data	Structured information
Finance	Sales data, expenses, bank transactions	Financial statements, budget reports, forecasts
Human Resources	Employee details, attendance, performance	Payroll, benefits management, performance reviews
Manufacturing	Inventory levels, production schedules	Production plans, material usage, work orders
Sales	Customer orders, product pricing	Sales trends, customer invoices, revenue analysis
Supply Chain	Supplier data, shipping records	Procurement reports, inventory management, logistics planning
Customer Relations	Customer interactions, service requests	Customer service reports, feedback analysis, issue resolution tracking
Project Management	Project timelines, resource allocation	Project progress reports, resource utilization, budget tracking

Table 3.6 ERP knowledge creation II (Author's work)

ERP module	Structured information	Knowledge	Type
Finance	Financial statements, budget reports, forecasts	Optimization of financial resources, investment strategies	Explicit
Human Resources	Payroll, benefits management, performance reviews	Enhanced HR policies, improved employee retention strategies	Tacit
Manufacturing	Production plans, material usage, work orders	Improved production techniques, cost reduction methods	Tacit
Sales	Sales trends, customer invoices, revenue analysis	Market trends understanding, customer needs assessment	Explicit
Supply Chain	Procurement reports, inventory management	Supply chain optimization, vendor management improvements	Tacit
Customer Relations	Customer service reports, feedback analysis	Customer satisfaction strategies, service improvement plans	Tacit
Project Management	Project progress reports, budget tracking	Project management methodologies, risk prevention strategies	Explicit

conditions and customer preferences, leading to explicit knowledge that can be directly applied to sales strategies. By studying procurement reports and inventory data, managers develop tacit knowledge about how to optimize the supply chain, which is often based on experience and know-how. Feedback and service reports lead to better understanding of customer needs and service gaps, resulting in tacit knowledge about how to enhance customer satisfaction. Tracking project progress and budget helps in forming explicit methodologies for managing projects more effectively, which can be codified, taught and repeated.

By processing structured information received from ERP modules managers and executives can utilize explicit, tacit or both types of knowledge to create further activities in order to improve operations and become more efficient.

3.6 Knowledge Management Life Cycle

Converting knowledge from the individual user to a group of users is one of the key issues in KM (O'Leary, 2002). There are different knowledge management life cycles proposed in IS projects. Wiig's KM cycle proposes four stages: building, holding, pooling and using knowledge (Wiig, 1994). Meyer and Zack (1996) knowledge management model consist of five stages: acquisition, storage/retrieval, distribution, presentation, refinement. Bukowitz and Williams (1999) use four stages: get, use, learn and contribute. Knowledge production and knowledge integration processes are used by McElroy KM cycle (McElroy, 2003). Dalkir (2005) proposed six stages: create/capture, assess, share, apply, contextualize and update. Evans and Ali (2013) knowledge management life cycle model have five stages: identify, organize and store, share, apply, evaluate and learn. Evans et al. (2014) built on Evans and Ali (2013) KM life cycle model to include the following stages: create or identify, store, share, use, learn and improve. Each of the stages proposed can be used in the ERP adoption process. Nakayama et al. (2021) used explicit and tacit knowledge to study system knowledge project outcomes in large scale information systems such as ERP. They mention that proper documentation is crucial for the success of the project.

McGinnis and Huang (2007) used revised SECI model and continues improvement model in order to incorporate KM into ERP project phases. The main part of this model is a supporting group that is assumed to be constant through all projects and phases. The main purpose of this group is to organize storing, generating, distributing and applying knowledge through the ERP cycle. They used four phases: analysis, design, deployment and construction. Each project where all four phases are complete represents one finished project. After first initial implementation of ERP all following module implementation would go through the same process and knowledge should be constant, properly managed by all users and support groups. Captured and stored knowledge should not be manipulated and conversion between explicit and tacit knowledge should be possible.

3.7 ERP Adoption Stages and KM Activities

The integration of KM into the ERP adoption process maximizes the effectiveness of the ERP across the business processes. In ERP adoption chapter we mentioned seven stages for successful ERP adoption. These stages are: pre-evaluation, evaluation and selection, project planning, GAP analysis, implementation, post-implementation and maintenance and update.

In the pre-evaluation stage important is to identify and collect present information about IS and HR assets. Our internal adoption team will be the main support team for knowledge management. Focus is on understanding and documenting how tasks/processes are performed, what are the inputs and outputs (incoming data for ERP and expected information from reports). The internal adoption team is taking feedback from experienced employees that are taking part in the process as well as those who are impacted by the outcome. Complete lists of current IT infrastructure, operational documents and system requirements is established. At this stage we are taking all present explicit knowledge in the form of documents, catalogs and procedures. This collected knowledge is reviewed and acknowledged as correct by the responsible employee. We are also identifying very special employees that are in possession of crucial knowledge for business processes. Knowledge sharing and capturing takes place as discussion among executive management and adoption team about existing bottlenecks, errors or delays in the process. Summary of KM activities in pre-evaluation stage and SECI representation is presented in Table 3.7.

In the evaluation stage the main purpose is to choose ERP solution that fits the best company's practices and goals. The KM activities include using the documents established in pre-evaluation stage and use it for further research and discussion

Table 3.7 Pre-evaluation phase KM activities (Author's work)

Pre-evaluation phase KM activities	Description	Knowledge type (SECI)
Identify and Collect IS and HR Asset Information	Gather detailed information about existing IS and HR assets. Create a list of current IT infrastructure including system and application manuals	Explicit to Explicit (C)
Business Processes	Understand and document how tasks and processes are performed. Collect feedback from experienced employees involved in the process and those impacted by the outcomes	Tacit to Explicit (E)
Review and Verify Knowledge	Ensure all collected knowledge, including documents, catalogs, and procedures, is reviewed and acknowledged as correct by responsible employees.	Explicit to Explicit (C)
Identify Key Knowledge Holders	Identify employees who possess crucial knowledge for business processes	Tacit to Tacit (S)
Facilitate Knowledge Sharing and Capturing	Conduct discussions among executive management and the adoption team to address existing bottlenecks, errors, or delays, and capture crucial knowledge from key employees	Tacit to Tacit (S) Tacit to Explicit (E)

with ERP vendors. Based on business needs, existing information about processes and projected budget internal adoption team define criteria for vendor evaluation. Vendor assessment and shortlisting is performed based on the vendor evaluation report. Through Request for Proposal process internal adoption team ask vendors to respond to our requirements and provide detailed proposal and quotation. After the internal adoption team received the proposal vendor presentations are executed to demonstrate functionalities according to specified RFP. Final discussion and negotiation based on quotation and recommendation from internal adoption team is performed by company executives. A summary of KM activities in the pre-evaluation stage and SECI representation is presented in Table 3.8.

In the project planning phase establishes proposed cross functional project team. Also, a detailed project plan is developed. Experienced project managers and key process users are involved in cross functional team development and project creation. Project risks are identified and according to them risk strategies and project protection plan are developed. Training and change management plan is developed to ensure well prepared training for end users of ERP modules. Summary of KM activities in project planning phase and SECI representation is presented in Table 3.9.

In GAP analysis the phase adoption team is identifying all gaps between the current state of performing business activities and proposed functionalities by the vendor. Analysis are performed by key process owners and adoption team (business analysts, department managers, ERP consultants, and vendor). Each identified gap should initiate a solution to overcome operational problems. Summary of KM activities in GAP analysis phase and SECI representation is presented in Table 3.10.

In the implementation phase most of the action and technical work takes place. It requires the involvement of all participants in the project and exchange of

Table 3.8 Evaluation phase KM activities (Author's work)

Evaluation phase KM activities	Description	Knowledge conversion type
Evaluation Documents	Use the documents established in the pre-evaluation stage for further research and discussion with ERP vendors	Explicit to Explicit (C)
Vendor Evaluation	Based on business needs, existing information about processes, and projected budget, the internal adoption team defines criteria for vendor evaluation	Explicit to Explicit (C)
Vendor Assessment and Shortlisting	Perform vendor assessment and shortlisting based on the vendor evaluation report	Explicit to Explicit (C)
Request for Proposal (RFP) Process	The internal adoption team create RFP and asks vendors to respond to our requirements and provide detailed proposals and quotations through the RFP process	Explicit to Explicit (C)
Vendor Presentations	After receiving the proposals, vendors are invited to execute presentations demonstrating functionalities according to the specified RFP	Tacit to Explicit (E)
Final Discussion and Negotiation	Company executives conduct final discussions and negotiations based on the quotation and recommendations from the internal adoption team	Explicit to Tacit (I)

Table 3.9 Project panning phase KM activities (Author's work)

Project planning phase KM activities	Description	Knowledge conversion type
Assembling the Project Team	Cross functional team establishment	Tacit to Tacit (S)
Developing a Project Plan	Developing timelines, milestones, resource allocations, and budgeting. The project plan also details specific steps and identifies potential risks	Tacit to Explicit (E) Explicit to Explicit (C)
Risk Management Strategies	Identify potential risks and protection strategies	Tacit to Explicit (E) Explicit to Explicit (C)
Change Management and Training Plans	Manage change and establish training programs for end users	Tacit to Explicit (E)

information and knowledge in different ways. Summary of KM activities in Implementation phase and SECI representation is presented in Table 3.11.

In the Post-Implementation stage the internal adoption team is focusing on internal continues improvement in operating ERP modules. New training material is developed by the adoption team, department managers and IT team. In the case of changes and training sessions organized with end users. If any changes are present to already explained work procedures the change is communicated to end users. All improvements in the ERP modules are recorded and documented. A summary of KM activities in Post-implementation phase and SECI representation is presented in Table 3.12.

Table 3.10 GAP analysis phase KM activities (Author's work)

GAP analysis phase KM activities	Description	Knowledge conversion type
Identifying Current Processes and Needs	Comparison of current state of processes. Capture of current ways of working in the system	Tacit to Explicit (E) Explicit to Explicit (C)
Mapping ERP Functionalities	Conduct mapping between ERP system functionalities and business processes and requirements	Tacit to Explicit (E) Explicit to Explicit (C)
Identifying Gaps	Identifying and recording gaps between the current processes and the selected ERP functionalities	Tacit to Explicit (E) Explicit to Explicit (C)
Developing Solutions for Gaps	Addressing each gap found and provide solutions. Initiating customization or process reengineering	Tacit to Explicit (E) Explicit to Explicit (C)

Table 3.11 Implementation Phase KM activities (Author's work)

Implementation phase KM activities	Description	Knowledge conversion type
System Setup and Configuration	Involves installing and configuring ERP application	Explicit to Explicit (C)
Data Migration	Importing of verified and checked information into the ERP database	Explicit to Explicit (C)
Customization and Integration	Updating code. Might involve best practices from experience	Tacit to Explicit (E)
Testing	Complete testing of all system functionalities and recording	Explicit to Explicit (C)
Training and Support	Ensures end-users are trained and ready to use ERP modules and features. Verbal training and training through manuals.	Tacit to Tacit (S) Explicit to Tacit (I)
Rollout	Begin using the system according to specifications	Explicit to Tacit (I)
Feedback and Optimization	Process owners collect feedback from end-users about the system's performance and share it with the adoption team. Feedback is recorded and communicated to vendor and consultants	Explicit to Explicit (C)

Last phase in the ERP adoption process is systems maintenance and update. In this phase we are continuously updating the procedures, performing system updates and making sure that ERP infrastructure, system software, security software and application software is up to date. This phase is mostly performed by IT team members and business analysts. Summary of KM activities in systems maintenance and update phase and SECI representation is presented in Table 3.13.

As suggested by Evans et al. (2014) KM cycle model includes the following stages: create or identify, store, share, use, learn and improve. Knowledge conversion types in each phase of ERP adoption process is different. Conversion very on the type of knowledge that has been transferred and also on type of participants

Table 3.12 ERP monitoring and optimization phase KM activities (Author's work)

ERP monitoring and optimization phase	Description	Knowledge conversion type
Continuous Training	New training material on new functionalities, procedures, and updates needs to be communicated to the adoption team and end users	Explicit to Tacit (I)
Change Management	Communication with managers and end users about changes in the roles and work routines	Tacit to Tacit (S)
Operations Strategy Alignment	Improvements to the ERP software through optimization or additional functionality development align with strategic operational decisions and workflows	Explicit to Explicit (C)

Table 3.13 System maintenance and update phase—KM activities (Author's work)

System maintenance and update phase—KM activities	Description	Knowledge conversion type
ERP Software Updates	Regular upgrades of functionalities, security and system software	Explicit to Explicit (C)
ERP Software Audit	Aligning ERP procedures with industry management standards	Explicit to Explicit (C)
ERP Monitoring and Process Evaluation	Ongoing monitoring and periodic audits of the ERP system	Explicit to Explicit (E)

included in the transfer of knowledge. Further this transfer depends on location where the original and new knowledge has been stored and how is it articulated. We defined the types of knowledge conversion and associating SECI dimension for each of the steps in ERP adoption process.

Analyzing KM spiral model of we can see constant transfer of knowledge and model stages throughout the ERP adoption process. Relating to McGinnis and Huang (2007) revised SECI model for integrating KM into ERP project phases we can agree on assumption that main supporting group that facilities knowledge management and knowledge transfer needs to be present. In our case this is adoption team. All members of the team should be involved in the project and should have a positive attitude for adoption. Knowledge, either tacit or explicit, is transferred throughout the phases of ERP adoption and new knowledge is created. The overall the most frequent type of conversion in the ERP adoption process is explicit to explicit which is combination followed by externalization, socialization and internalization dimension from SECI model. New knowledge should be documented and stored either in ERP database or KMS repositories. Integration of KMS functionalities and ERP modules is not part of this chapter but adoption steps can be followed in the KMS adoption cases.

3.8 Conclusions

Most of the medium and large companies are using ERP modules and follow KM strategies to stay competitive. Adoption of ERP systems bring many benefits to organizations if adopted and implemented properly. Knowledge management is seen through many definitions. Overall, it is a continuous process of knowledge identification, storage, transfer, new knowledge creation and usage. Knowledge types present in ERP adoption process is explicit, tacit and embedded. Knowledge creation is supported by ERP through processing raw data using different modules. Structured information is further used either by modules or by individuals to create organizational knowledge. In each phase of the adoption process different activities are performed. The knowledge conversion process is present and continuous through all of the stages. All four dimensions of knowledge conversion are used throughout the ERP adoption stages. This chapter reflects on previous findings in the KM and ERP adoption field and can be used by the companies that are in the process of adopting ERP solutions or integrating ERP and KM practices.

References

Alavi, M., & Leidner, D. (1999). Knowledge management systems: Issues, challenges, and benefits. *Communications of the Association for Information Systems, 1*(1), 7.

Bukowitz, W. R., & Williams, R. L. (1999). *The knowledge management fieldbook*. Financial Times Prentice Hall.

Burk, M. (1999). Cycle of knowledge. *Public Roads, 63*, 26.

Chang, I., Li, Y., Hung, W., & Hwang, H. (2005). An empirical study on the impact of quality antecedents on tax payers' acceptance of internet tax-filing systems. *Government Information Quarterly, 22*(3), 389–410.

Chou, H. W., Lin, Y. H., Lu, H. S., Chang, H. H., & Chou, S. B. (2014). Knowledge sharing and ERP system usage in post-implementation stage. *Computers in Human Behavior, 33*, 16–22.

Cianciolo, A. T., Matthew, C., Sternberg, R. J., & Wagner, R. K. (2006). Tacit knowledge, practical intelligence, and expertise. *The Cambridge handbook of expertise and expert performance* (pp. 613–632).

Dalkir, K. (2005). *Knowledge management in theory and practice*. Elsevier.

Davenport, T. H. (1998). Putting the enterprise into the enterprise system. *Harvard Business Review, 76*(4), 121–131.

Davenport, T., De Long, D., & Beers, M. (1998). Successful knowledge management projects. *Sloan Management Review, 39*(2), 43–57.

DeLone, W. H., & McLean, E. R. (1992). Information systems success: The quest for the dependent variable. *Information Systems Research, 3*(1), 60–95.

Evans, M. M., & Ali, N. (2013, October). Bridging knowledge management life cycle theory and practice. In *International conference on intellectual capital, knowledge management and Organisational learning ICICKM 2013–conference proceedings* (pp. 156–165).

Evans, M., Dalkir, K., & Bidian, C. (2014). A holistic view of the knowledge life cycle: The knowledge management cycle (KMC) model. *Electronic Journal of Knowledge Management, 12*(2), 85–97.

Fan, J. C., & Fang, K. (2006). ERP implementation and information systems success: A test of DeLone and McLean's model. In *2006 Technology Management for the Global Future-PICMET 2006 conference* (Vol. 3, pp. 1272–1278). IEEE.
Gamble, P. R., & Blackwell, J. (2001). *Knowledge management: A state of the art guide.*
Gunasekaran, A., Ngai, E. W., & Cheng, T. E. (2007). Developing an e-logistics system: A case study. *International Journal of Logistics, 10*(4), 333–349.
Huber, G. P. (2001). Transfer of knowledge in knowledge management systems: Unexplored issues and suggested studies. *European Journal of Information Systems, 10*(2), 72–79.
Hwang, H. I. (2008). Investigation of the application of KMS for disease classification> a studz in a Taiwanese hospital. *Expert Systems with Applications, 34*(1), 725–733.
Jones, M. (2005). Tacit knowledge sharing during ERP implementation: A multi-site case study. *Information Resources Management Journal (IRMJ), 18*(2), 1–23.
Karim, M. R., Nordin, N., Yusof, M. F., Amin, M. B., Islam, M. A., & Hassan, M. S. (2023). Does ERP implementation mediate the relationship between knowledge management and the perceived organizational performance of the healthcare sector? Evidence from a developing country. *Cogent Business & Management, 10*(3), 2275869.
Kuo, R., & Lee, G. (2009). KMS adoption: The effects of information quality. *Management Decision, 47*(10), 1633–1651.
Lee, Z., & Lee, J. (2000). An ERP implementation case study from a knowledge transfer perspective. *Journal of Information Technology, 15*(4), 281–288.
Mahendrawathi, E. R. (2015). Knowledge management support for enterprise resource planning implementation. *Procedia Computer Science, 72*, 613–621.
Markus, M. L., & Tanis, C. (2000). The enterprise systems experience-from adoption to success. *Framing the Domains of IT Research: Glimpsing the Future Through the Past, 173*(2000), 207–173.
McElroy, M. W. (2003). Understanding "the new knowledge management". *Long Range Planning, 30*(3), 374–384.
McGinnis, T. C., & Huang, Z. (2007). Rethinking ERP success: A new perspective from knowledge management and continuous improvement. *Information & Management, 44*(7), 626–634.
Meyer, M., & Zack, M. (1996). The design and implementation of information products. *Sloan Management Review, 37*(3), 43–59.
Nakayama, M., Hustad, E., & Sutcliffe, N. (2021). Agility and system documentation in large-scale enterprise system projects: A knowledge management perspective. *Procedia Computer Science, 181*, 386–393.
Nonaka, I., & Takeuchi, H. (2001). Organizational knowledge creation. *Creative management, 64.*
Nonaka, L., Takeuchi, H., & Umemoto, K. (1996). A theory of organizational knowledge creation. *International Journal of Technology Management, 11*(7–8), 833–845.
O'Leary, D. E. (2002). Knowledge management across the enterprise resource planning systems life cycle. *International Journal of Accounting Information Systems, 3*(2), 99–110.
Oxford University Press Staff, & Berkley Publishing Group. (2001). *The Oxford American desk dictionary and thesaurus*. Berkley.
Parry, G., & Graves, A. (2008). The importance of knowledge management for ERP systems. *International Journal of Logistics: Research and Applications, 11*(6), 427–441.
Polanyi, M. (1966). The logic of tacit inference. *Philosophy, 41*(155), 1–18.
Stanciu, V., & Tinca, A. (2013). ERP solutions-catalyts for the companies' business. *CAL, 14*, 170.
Turulja, L., & Bajgorić, N. (2018). Knowledge acquisition, knowledge application, and innovation towards the ability to adapt to change. *International Journal of Knowledge Management (IJKM), 14*(2), 1–15.
Wagner, R. K., & Sternberg, R. J. (1985). Practical intelligence in real-world pursuits: The role of tacit knowledge. *Journal of Personality and Social Psychology, 49*(2), 436.
Wiig, K. M. (1994). *Knowledge management foundations: Thinking about thinking-how people and organizations represent, create, and use knowledge*. Schema Press.

Wu, J. H., & Wang, Y. M. (2006). Measuring KMS success: A respecification of the DeLone and McLean's model. *Information & Management, 43*(6), 728–739.

Xu, L., Wang, C., Luo, X., & Shi, Z. (2006). Integrating knowledge management and ERP in enterprise information systems. *Systems Research and Behavioral Science: The Official Journal of the International Federation for Systems Research, 23*(2), 147–156.

Zhou, T., Li, H., & Liu, Y. (2010). The effect of flow experience on mobile SNS users' loyalty. *Industrial Management & Data Systems, 110*(6), 930–946.

Chapter 4
ERP Systems, Knowledge Management and Organizational Performance

4.1 Introduction

Enterprise resource planning (ERP) systems are essential to increasing organizational capabilities and streamlining business processes in the ever-changing business technology environment. Key performance indicators can be greatly impacted by thoughtful alignment of ERP system integration with company objectives. With ERP systems attracting large investments and divergent information on their efficacy, it is important to critically examine how these systems impact different facets of corporate and organizational performance.

Moreover, it is hard to overstate how important knowledge management is to this analysis. An ERP system can be effectively implemented to greatly enhance the efficient handling and distribution of information and expertise inside an organization, which is made possible by knowledge management (KM).

The fundamental function of ERP systems in streamlining and integrating business processes and data across the organization is where the link between them, along with knowledge management and organizational performance, makes sense. Through ensuring that information is available and regularly shared across departments, this centralized and integrated system enhances knowledge management and promotes better communication and decision-making. Through the more effective execution of processes, the reduction of errors, and the guarantee that staff members have instant access to the information they need, such integration of information systems enhances organizational performance. Therefore, ERP systems function as the foundation for knowledge management practices, which through increased operational effectiveness and decision-making capacity, enhance organizational performance (Jayawickrama et al., 2017). Furthermore, Acar et al. (2017) describe how ERP systems facilitate data and process management by serving as a central repository that guarantees timely, accurate, and pertinent information availability across the company. Then, by building on this foundation, knowledge management

L. Turulja et al., *Integrating ERP Systems and Knowledge Management*, Progress in IS, https://doi.org/10.1007/978-3-031-68922-2_4

practices help to generate, share, and apply knowledge, which enhances creativity and decision-making. Effectively, KM leverages this structured information to enhance organizational capabilities and performance, even as ERP systems serve as the foundation of data and process management. This synergy is especially noticeable in the way that KM practices can mediate the connection between operational performance and ERP implementation, showing that the value of ERP is maximized when connected to strategic knowledge management initiatives.

The link between ERP systems and knowledge management techniques as well as between ERP and organizational performance are discussed in the text that follows.

4.2 Methodological Approach and Research Objectives

To explore the relationship between ERP and organisational performance, as well as relationship between ERP and KM, a Systematic Literature Review (SLR) will be conducted. Methodologically speaking, SLR seeks to compile, assess critically, and summarize all pertinent research on a certain subject or issue in order to guarantee a thorough and objective analysis. Given the abundance of research in a field, this approach is especially helpful in summarizing the body of knowledge and pointing up gaps (Torres-Carrion et al., 2018).

The aim of this research is to find out whether ERP systems improve company performance and how knowledge management and ERP interact. The Web of Science Core Collection will be used in a methodical literature search to accomplish a comprehensive review.

The most current and pertinent scholarly contributions to the subject were included by conducting this search on May 14, 2024. By means of this SLR, the research seeks to outline the data regarding the influence of ERP systems on company performance, as well as the relationship between ERP and KM.

Bibliographic analysis is also applied to map the research domains according to keyword co-occurrence. Examining vast volumes of scientific data is a common use of bibliometric analysis techniques. It enables us to explore the particulars of a certain area's development and draws attention to fresh and developing subjects in that field (Donthu et al., 2021). It is a method that examines publication metadata, such as titles, abstracts, and keywords, to identify patterns, trends, and relationships within the academic literature (Lim & Buntine, 2016). Through the disclosure of the frequency and association of particular terms in a data set, this method can illuminate the evolution and relationship between concepts and themes over time. Analysing these trends allows one to create a thorough picture of the subject, pointing up important themes, influential research, and possible gaps in the literature.

4.3 ERP Systems and Organizational Performance

ERPs are key tools for improving organizational capabilities, directly influencing business processes and performance results. An SLR approach was used in data collecting and study selection to better comprehend the relationship between ERP systems and organizational performance. The procedure of identifying studies and analyzing them in order to map the research area is described in the text below.

4.3.1 *Data Collection and Study Selection*

The following search string was constructed to capture the most relevant studies on the relationship between ERP and business performance:

"Enterprise Resource Planning" OR ERP OR "enterprise application" (Title) AND "organi*ational performance" OR "business performance" OR "company performance" OR "firm performance" OR "financial performance" OR "operational performance" (Topic) and English (Languages)*

The objectives of this SLR on the relationship between ERP systems and business or organizational performance are as follows:

- Identify and map the body of research on the impact of ERP systems on business and organizational performance, categorizing studies by key words.
- Analyse how ERP systems contribute to specific aspects of business performance.

There were 117 documents found overall between 2000 and 2024 using the previously specified search string. Articles: 114, and review articles: 3, early access: 1 are the categories under which downloaded documents are filed.

With its thorough search of a large amount of literature, this study offers a strong basis for evaluating how ERP systems affect company performance.

From 2000 to 2024, the trend in publications and citations on enterprise resource planning and its effect on organizational or business performance is shown in Fig. 4.1. Its increasing number of publications and citations over time demonstrates the expanding relevance and academic interest in this field of study. Few publications at first, with a steady rise in citations, that represented the basic development of research over time. The peak of publications and the citations that follow indicate that research output and its influence peaked around 2021. This tendency emphasizes how ERP research is becoming more and more important in academic and practical domains in tandem with organizational needs and technology advancement.

The results indicate a wide range of publications in several scientific fields, underscoring the interdisciplinary interest in the connection between organizational or business performance and enterprise resource planning (ERP). With 42 records, "Management" is the biggest category; "Informatics, library science" and "Information systems of computing" follow with 23 and 31 records, respectively.

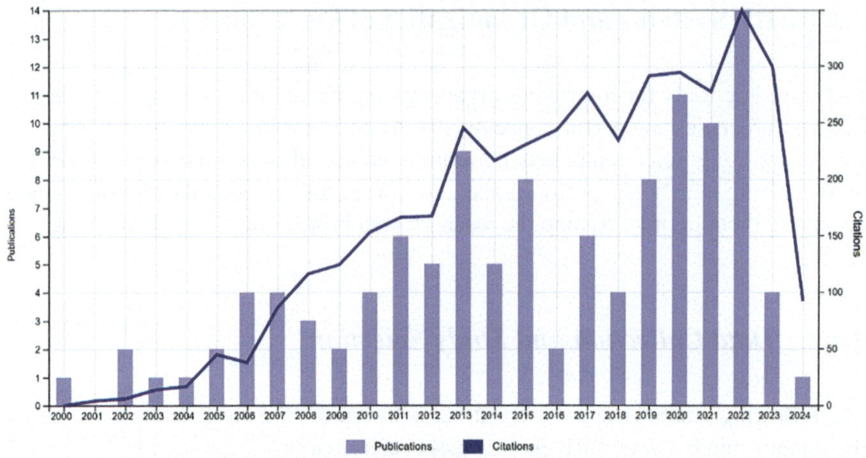

Fig. 4.1 Times cited and publications over time. Source: Web of Science

Important but minor categories are "Business," "Engineering," and "Operations research management science." Categories including "Environmental Sciences," "Environmental Studies," and "Green sustainable science technology" also include environmental thought. This broad spectrum of categories reflects important interest in and research activity from many academic and practical viewpoints.

4.3.2 Data Analysis and Results Discussion

Using the bibliometric analysis program VosViewer, a thorough bibliographic analysis was carried forth. A technique used in literature reviews, bibliographic analysis methodically looks through books, scholarly articles, and other sources. It comprises different approaches for mapping and assessing the breadth, depth, and kind of research activity. Significant patterns in the body of knowledge under review can be found with the aid of this procedure. Important for comprehending how a research area develops over time, it facilitates the identification of significant studies and new directions by researchers. VosViewer is bibliometric network construction and visualization software that links journals, researchers, or individual articles according to shared characteristics like citations, references, or keywords. Especially helpful is this tool for graphically examining relationships and main ideas in a large body of literature.

First, using author keywords (minimum number of occurrences: 7) a co-occurrence analysis was done. Three different clusters were found by this analysis; these are shown in Fig. 4.2.

Three unique clusters of keywords that stand for thematic areas in ERP research are displayed on the co-occurrence analysis map. Establishing these clusters offers

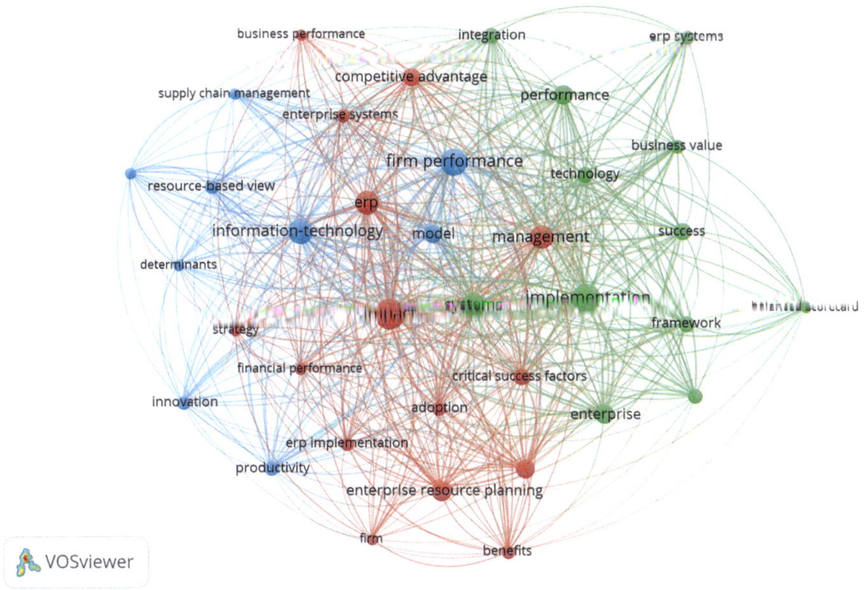

Fig. 4.2 Keywords co-occurence map

a systematic summary of the subject and emphasizes the various ways that ERP systems affect various aspects of organizational performance.

- **Red cluster** (Impact): This cluster is concerned with the several stages and deliverables of ERP implementation. Emphasizing important terms like "ERP implementation" and "adoption," which point to a concentration on the procedural and practical components of implementing ERP systems inside organizations, it encapsulates the core of the ERP adoption process. The terms "impact" and "benefits" highlight how these systems affect the effectiveness and efficiency of organizations. This cluster probably represents research that look at the implementation of ERP systems: the difficulties and achievements as well as the real effects on the operations and performance of organizations.
- **Green cluster** (Implementation and integration): This cluster emphasizes the strategic frameworks and approaches used in the integration of ERP systems into organizational structures. Terms that point to an emphasis on the planning and systems aspects of ERP include "enterprise resource planning" and "ERP systems." "Framework" and "implementation" indicate the methodical methods needed for an ERP implementation to be successful. Words like "integration" and "systems" imply that ERP's technical components, such as how those systems interface with the company's current technology, will take center stage. The use of "business value" and "balanced results" suggests a desire in using strategic performance management tools to quantify and control the effect of ERP systems. This cluster probably includes research on the theoretical and practical

frameworks that facilitate ERP integration and assess how well it enhances organizational performance.

- **Blue cluster** (Information technology and performance): This cluster specializes on the theoretical underpinnings and performance results of ERP systems, concentrating especially on how these systems impact performance at the enterprise-level. ERP systems are supposed to provide both operational and strategic advantages, as seen by terms like "firm performance," "productivity," and "supply chain management". "Determinants" and "model" point to a curiosity in the theories and elements influencing the effective implementation and use of ERP systems. A "resource-based view" means that some research in this cluster looks at ERP from a strategic management angle, looking at how ERP systems can offer competitive advantages depending on the resources and capabilities of a company. The terms "information technology" and "cloud ERP" capture the technological development of ERP systems, particularly the shift to cloud-based solutions, which may be connected to research on innovation and ERP technology advancement. This cluster probably contains research that look into how to use cutting-edge technology and efficient resource management to enhance different facets of company performance in addition to what makes ERP implementations successful.

The purpose of this study was to identify and map research literature on the influence of ERP systems on organizational and business performance, with a particular emphasis on the classification of the research by pertinent keywords. Three primary clusters were identified by this methodical approach; each cluster represents a significant facet of ERP research and its consequences for organizational dynamics. The results demonstrate that three subthemes of subfields can be successfully separated into the research field examining the relationship between ERP systems and organizational performance. The first subfield addresses the whole ERP implementation life cycle, from the first adoption procedure to the ultimate effects on the company. Studies in this field usually look into the benefits and difficulties of ERP system implementation as well as the operational processes and results. The second subfield is centered on ERP system integration techniques and strategic frameworks. This entails delving deeply into the architecture and implementation of ERP systems inside current organizational procedures and technology. Here, the strategic and technological components of ERP systems that guarantee their effective deployment and operational alignment with company objectives are the main emphasis. The third subfield finally addresses the performance outcomes and theoretical underpinnings of ERP systems. This includes examining the effects of these systems on corporate performance and innovation. Research that reflects both the technical developments and strategic management viewpoints that propel ERP success frequently looks at how ERP systems can be used to boost productivity and competitive advantage.

Several highly influential studies that shed light on various facets of ERP implementation and results document the scientific landscape of enterprise resource planning and its effect on organizational performance, as depicted in Table 4.1.

Table 4.1 Most cited documents (more than 100 citations)

Title	Authors and publication year	Source title	Total citations	Average per year
Investment in Enterprise Resource Planning: Business impact and productivity measures	Hitt et al. (2002)	Journal of Management Information Systems	429	18.65
Learning from adopters' experiences with ERP: Problems encountered and success achieved	Markus et al. (2000)	Journal of Information Technology	359	14.36
Enterprise resource planning (ERP) competence constructs: Two-stage multi-item scale development and validation	Stratman and Roth (2002)	Decision Sciences	223	9.7
ERP systems adoption: An exploratory study of the organizational factors and impacts of ERP success	Law and Ngai (2007)	Information & Management	181	10.06
The role of information systems resources in ERP capability building and business process outcomes	Karimi et al. (2007)	Journal of Management Information Systems	141	7.83
Implementation critical success factors (CSFs) for ERP: Do they contribute to implementation success and post-implementation performance?	Ram et al. (2013)	International Journal of Production Economics	125	10.42

Understanding the direct advantages of ERP systems turned out to be crucial, and one of the most cited papers is Hitt et al. (2002) study on the business impact and productivity measures related with ERP investments. The user experiences research by Markus et al. (2000) provides insightful information about the difficulties and achievements of ERP implementation, which is useful for next implementations. The ERP competency scale was created to help measure the abilities needed to use an ERP system efficiently (Stratman & Roth, 2002). Research by Law and Ngai (2007), as well as Karimi et al. (2007) explores the strategic management of information systems resources to enhance ERP capabilities as well as the organizational elements influencing ERP success. Furthermore, a comprehensive analysis of what leads to successful ERP implementation and long-term performance advantages is provided by Ram et al. (2013) analysis of critical success factors.

4.3.3 *Analyzing ERP Systems' Impact on Business Performance Across Key Domains*

Because ERP provide a multi-layered platform that enhances performance across many organizational functions, they are essential to modern business management. In order to produce a more effective and streamlined working environment, these systems integrate and automate key business processes including finance, human resources, manufacturing, supply chain, and customer service. Financial results, operational effectiveness, customer satisfaction, and strategic decision-making are all profoundly and variably impacted by ERP systems. ERP systems support strategic alignment with market dynamics, enable better resource management, and deliver vital insights and analytics by offering a centralized and linked data environment.

First of all, by integrating financial data, enhancing accuracy, and guaranteeing compliance, ERP systems affect financial results. Better financial planning and in real time financial reporting are made possible by the integration of financial operations with other business processes. As stressed by Law and Ngai (2007), ERP systems enhance financial control and transparency, which are essential for prompt decision-making and financial health monitoring. Moreover, the automation and optimization of company procedures made possible by ERP systems raises the operational efficiency of companies. ERP systems reduce operating costs and increase efficiency by integrating several functions including manufacturing, logistics, and inventory management (Stratman & Roth, 2002). By guaranteeing a seamless information flow across the company, this integration lowers delays and gets rid of duplicates. Customer satisfaction can also be greatly impacted by ERP systems since they guarantee effective and quick processes that interact with customers. By better controlling inventory and manufacturing schedules, ERP systems, for instance, can shorten delivery times and raise the standard of services. By means of enhanced demand forecasting and customer relationship management, ERP systems, according to Law and Ngai (2007), support higher service levels and increased customer satisfaction. Additionally, by offering thorough, correct, and current data that facilitates long-term planning and market analysis, ERP systems support strategic decision-making. ERP systems enable companies to swiftly adjust to market changes and opportunities by coordinating IT capabilities with business strategies, as discussed by Stratman and Roth (2002). Innovation is fostered and competitive advantage is maintained only by this strategic alignment. The general advantages and difficulties of putting an ERP system into place inside businesses are covered by Beheshti and Beheshti (2010). Emphasizing ERP as a crucial instrument for combining different business processes, the talk emphasizes how it can increase productivity and general performance of the company. Among the main advantages mentioned are higher output, lower running expenses, and happier customers. They do caution about difficulties, though, such a large initial outlay and the need for efficient change management to get over internal opposition.

When it comes to recent studies, a study by Nour (2023) looks into how contextual and antecedent variables affect the advantages of an ERP system and how these advantages impact the performance of the organization. The outcomes validate how important ERP/organizational alignment and business process reengineering are for enhancing intra-organizational coordination, integration, and data and information quality. Through data and information quality in particular, these enhancements have been demonstrated to enhance organizational performance; however, the study did not find a statistically significant impact of better coordination alone on performance. Using a technology-organization-environment (TOE) framework, Lutfi et al. (2022) look into the elements affecting ERP system adoption and perceived benefits at the organizational level. Their results show that while compatibility was unexpectedly insignificant, technological factors like the ERP system's relative advantage have a big impact on adoption. ERP adoption was more likely when top management support, the organization was prepared, and there was thorough training. Furthermore, important roles were played by environmental elements including government rules and competitive pressure. To fully benefit from ERP, especially in enhancing business performance and competitiveness among SMEs, this study emphasizes the complexity of ERP adoption and the need of coordinating organizational and technological strategies. TQM and ERP both greatly and favorably impact organizational performance, according to Al-Dhaafri and Alosani (2022). Above all, the study reveals that organizational performance acts as a mediator between TQM, ERP, and organizational excellence. This suggests that the way that TQM and ERP implementation affect organizational performance greatly influences their ability to enhance organizational excellence. This study not only emphasizes the specific contributions of ERP systems and TQM to performance but also emphasizes the need of raising overall organizational performance as a mediator for attaining higher organizational excellence.

4.4 ERP Systems and Knowledge Management

ERP systems help to improve different organizational capabilities, of which knowledge management (KM) is a well-known field acknowledged in scientific literature. As was already indicated, the SLR approach was used to gather data and choose studies in order to look into the connection between ERP systems and knowledge management. The following paper explains the process of finding and evaluating pertinent research in order to make the connection between knowledge management and ERP clearer.

4.4.1 Data Collection and Study Selection

The following search string was constructed to capture the most relevant studies on the relationship between ERP and knowledge management:

"Enterprise Resource Planning" OR ERP OR "enterprise application" (Title) AND "knowledge management" (Topic) and English (Languages)*

The objectives of this SLR on the relationship between ERP systems and knowledge management are as follows:

- Identify and map the body of research on the relationship between ERP systems and knowledge management, categorizing studies by key words.
- Analyze how ERP systems contribute to specific practices of knowledge management.

Using the previously defined search string, a total of 57 documents in English from the period 2001 to 2024 were identified. Downloaded documents are categorized as follows: articles: 54, and review articles: 3.

The publication and citation trend for the field pertaining to the connection between ERP and KM is shown in Fig. 4.3 over the period of 2001–2023.

There are yearly publications displayed in a bar graph. The quantity of articles is increasing gradually, which suggests that this field is becoming more and more interesting. The number of publications appears to fluctuate after 2013, which could mean that by then, basic elements of the relationship between ERP and KM had been established, and that later works would have concentrated on improving theories, techniques, or technology. The number of citations these publications receive annually is shown in a line chart. Citations, interestingly, peak later than publications, most obviously between 2018 and 2020. A few high-impact publications that

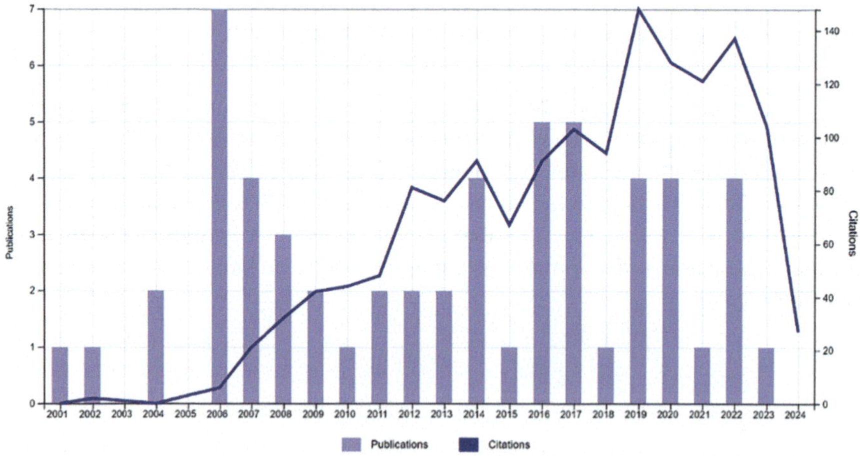

Fig. 4.3 Times cited and publications over time. Source: Web of Science

raise awareness of the field or foundational papers published in earlier years that gained recognition could be reflected in a citation peak.

Quantified by the number of contributions or studies in each area, the largest area, "Management," with 21 contributions, denotes the main area of research focus in the study of ERP and KM. Further noteworthy contributions from "Computer science information systems" (16 contributions) and "Library information science" (9 contributions) point to a robust multidisciplinary approach combining these disciplines. Littler sections cover subjects like "engineering," "operations research management science," and "computer science" (including artificial intelligence and multidisciplinary applications).

4.4.2 Data Analysis and Results Discussion

Using the bibliometric analysis program VosViewer, a bibliographic analysis was carried forth. Author keywords were used to first do a co-occurrence analysis (three occurrences minimum). Three different clusters were found by this analysis; Fig. 4.4 shows them off.

Three separate clusters of keywords that stand in for thematic areas are displayed on the co-occurrence study map. Establishing these clusters offers a systematic summary of the subject and emphasizes the connections between knowledge management practices and ERP.

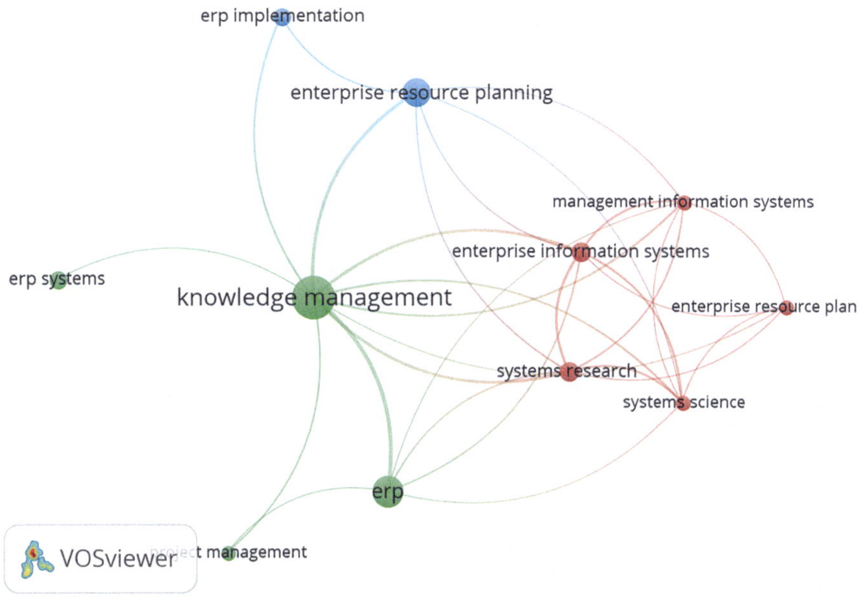

Fig. 4.4 Keywords co-occurence map

- **Red cluster** (ERP and information systems research): The integration and operation of the ERP system within the larger framework of the information systems of the organization are the topics of this cluster. It underlines how important ERP systems are to centralizing and streamlining company operations, which makes better knowledge management and decision-making possible. The cluster also looks at how management information systems (MIS) affect the best way to implement and use ERP. Moreover, it includes systems science and research, which offer a more comprehensive knowledge of the technological frameworks and system interactions supporting ERP systems, guaranteeing that they successfully support organizational objectives and knowledge sharing.
- **Green cluster** (ERP implementation and Knowledge management): This cluster concerned with the complementary effects of combining ERP systems with knowledge management practices in businesses. It makes clear that knowledge management efficiency can be greatly increased by ERP systems by centralizing and streamlining data and procedures. Through the provision of thorough, pertinent information to all departments, this integration promotes improved decision-making, project management, and organizational learning. Moreover, the cluster emphasizes the need of project management in the effective implementation of ERP systems to maximize knowledge flows and raise general corporate performance. Enterprises wishing to use their combined knowledge and data to obtain a competitive advantage must understand how ERP systems and knowledge management interact.
- **Blue cluster** (ERP implementation): This cluster focuses on important features of ERP and how companies implement it. Emphasizing the need for careful planning and management to fully benefit ERP systems for rationalizing organizational workflows and improving operational efficiency, this focus on both the theory and practical implementation of ERP highlights the complexities and challenges involved in ERP implementation, including system selection, customization, user training, and long-term support.

Three narrowly oriented subthemes can be distinguished in the literature examining the relationship between ERP systems and knowledge management. The first subtheme, which focuses on how ERP systems are included into larger organizational information systems, highlights how they help to improve decision-making and knowledge sharing as well as streamline operations. The second sub-theme demonstrates how ERP systems enhance data centralization and enable comprehensive knowledge management, which facilitates better decision-making and project management, and so highlights the synergistic effects of ERP systems on organizational knowledge practices. The third subtheme, which focuses on the crucial elements of project execution and management required to use ERP systems for best operational efficiency and knowledge management integration, finally looks at the particular difficulties and complexities involved in the practical implementation of ERP systems. These three subthemes taken together cover the broad influence of ERP systems on the enhancement and control of knowledge inside companies.

The most referenced articles are listed in Table 4.2. They all address different aspects of ERP implementation and how it relates to knowledge management. Using service quality as their focus, Hsu et al. (2015) evaluate ERP success at the individual level after implementation. With more than 103 citations, this paper emphasizes the need of user satisfaction and service quality in assessing ERP success by providing a detailed viewpoint on individual effects instead of general organizational measures. Another study, cited 99 times, is Beheshti and Beheshti (2010), which links ERP implementation directly to improved productivity and performance metrics inside firms. This paper has had a significant impact in relating ERP systems to observable business results and offers academics and practitioners trying to defend ERP expenditures with a useful reference. With their unique perspective on knowledge management integration within ERP systems, Xu et al. (2006) show how these systems can act as a hub for both data management and organizational knowledge processes. Awa and Ojiabo (2016) also examined the adoption determinants of ERP within a Technology-Organization-Environment (T-O-E) framework and were cited 85 times for their extensive model that predicts and improves the success of ERP implementations depending on organizational, technological, and environmental aspects.

Table 4.2 Most cited documents (more than 60 citations)

Title	Authors and publication year	Source title	Total citations	Average per year
Assessing ERP post-implementation success at the individual level: Revisiting the role of service quality	Hsu et al. (2015)	Information & Management	103	10.3
Improving productivity and firm performance with enterprise resource planning	Beheshti and Beheshti (2010)	Enterprise Information Systems	99	6.6
Integrating knowledge management and ERP in enterprise information systems	Xu et al. (2006)	Systems Research and Behavioral Science	96	5.05
A model of adoption determinants of ERP within T-O-E framework	Awa and Ojiabo (2016)	Information Technology & People	85	9.44
Rethinking ERP success: A new perspective from knowledge management and continuous improvement	McGinnis and Huang (2007)	Information & Management	78	4.33
Sustainable enterprise resource planning: imperatives and research directions	Chofreh et al. (2014)	Journal of Cleaner Production	74	6.73
The role of organizational knowledge management in successful ERP implementation projects	Vandaie (2008)	Knowledge-based Systems	65	3.82

By illuminating the intricate and multidimensional character of ERP systems in organizational contexts, these studies taken together provide important new perspectives on the implementation, perception, and application of these systems to enhance performance and efficiently handle knowledge. This scientific conversation aids in comprehending the direct and indirect advantages of ERP systems and in pointing up the ongoing enhancements and calculated interactions required to optimize their value.

4.4.3 Analyzing ERP Systems' Impact on Knowledge Management

By concentrating on how the several aspects of service quality, system quality, and information quality impact user satisfaction and extended system use, Hsu et al. (2015) offer an in-depth analysis of post-implementation ERP success. Through highlighting the value of extended use—that is, using a larger range of ERP features for better knowledge use, they demonstrate how ERP systems support knowledge management. The report emphasizes the critical importance of service quality, pointing out that better user engagement and system effectiveness are facilitated by better knowledge sharing and management by better IT staff support. Furthermore, user interaction with the ERP system and satisfaction are greatly influenced by the interaction between high system and information quality, which encourages more efficient knowledge management procedures inside the company. Stated differently, the study establishes a clear connection between the technical capabilities and service aspects of ERP systems and their capacity to facilitate and enhance knowledge management activities inside companies (Hsu et al., 2015). Through the integration of business processes, ERP can improve productivity and performance, as Beheshti and Beheshti (2010) discuss. Through their support of decision-making processes, availability and accuracy of data, and ability to facilitate the seamless flow of information across all business functions, ERP systems enhance knowledge management. Through the facilitation of knowledge sharing and efficient use, this integration promotes ongoing advancement of organizational learning and operational effectiveness. Through their promotion of ERP systems' integration into corporate information systems, Xu et al. (2006) look into how they support knowledge management practices. They discuss how integrating KM and ERP systems enhances a company's capacity to efficiently manage its knowledge and physical resources, so enhancing its competitive advantage. Traditionally concentrating on data and process simplification for operational effectiveness, ERP systems offer a strong foundation for the knowledge processes necessary for knowledge management (KM), including the gathering, storing, sharing, and application of knowledge across the company. When KM is included into ERP, the systems' capabilities are expanded beyond their traditional functions to include support for ongoing learning and innovation inside companies. By strategically leveraging the data produced by ERP, this synergy turns transactional data into knowledge that can be applied to process improvement and decision-making. ERP systems also help to record and distribute tacit knowledge, which enhances organizational learning and flexibility. Organizations may achieve a more comprehensive approach to management that targets operational efficiency and promotes an environment of continuous improvement and knowledge-driven growth by implementing ERP and KM concurrently (Xu et al., 2006).

When it comes to more recent studies, Karim et al. (2023) look at how ERP implementation in the healthcare industry serves as a mediator between knowledge management practices and perceived organizational performance. It concludes that by enhancing the generation, distribution, and application of knowledge, ERP systems support knowledge management and so enhance organizational effectiveness. ERP systems facilitate the efficient information flow that facilitates improved decision-making and operational performance by centralizing data and simplifying procedures. Khalilzadeh and Alikhani (2020) demonstrate how ensuring structured and standardized project management through ERP implementation enhances knowledge management practices by integrating Project Management Body of Knowledge standards. By precisely managing and applying knowledge at various phases of ERP implementation, this methodical approach guarantees that knowledge is efficiently gathered, shared, and applied, so enhancing overall project success and organizational learning. Through professionalization and effective application of knowledge, ERP systems help SMEs manage their knowledge (Heredia-Calzado & Duréndez, 2019). This demonstrates how professionalization, especially through focused training, gives staff members the abilities they need to use ERP systems to their full potential, which promotes better information flow and strategic decision making. By matching corporate operations with the knowledge objectives of the company, this integration of ERP systems with knowledge management techniques maximizes operational efficiency and offers a competitive advantage.

References

Acar, M. F., Tarim, M., Zaim, H., Zaim, S., & Delen, D. (2017). Knowledge management and ERP: Complementary or contradictory? *International Journal of Information Management, 37*(6), 703–712. https://doi.org/10.1016/j.ijinfomgt.2017.05.007

Al-Dhaafri, H. S., & Alosani, M. S. (2022). The intermediary role of organizational performance as a driver of total quality management and enterprise resource planning towards achieving organizational excellence: The moderating role of demographic factors. *The TQM journal, 34*(5), 1226–1249.

Awa, H. O., & Ojiabo, O. U. (2016). A model of adoption determinants of ERP within T-O-E framework. *Information Technology and People, 29*(4), 901–930. https://doi.org/10.1108/ITP-03-2015-0068

Beheshti, H. M., & Beheshti, C. M. (2010). Improving productivity and firm performance with enterprise resource planning. *Enterprise Information Systems, 4*(4), 445–472. https://doi.org/10.1080/17517575.2010.511276

Chofreh, A. G., Goni, F. A., Shaharoun, A. M., Ismail, S., & Klemeš, J. J. (2014). Sustainable enterprise resource planning: Imperatives and research directions. *Journal of Cleaner Production, 71*, 139–147. https://doi.org/10.1016/j.jclepro.2014.01.010

Donthu, N., Kumar, S., Mukherjee, D., Pandey, N., & Lim, W. M. (2021). How to conduct a bibliometric analysis: An overview and guidelines. *Journal of Business Research, 133*, 285–296. https://doi.org/10.1016/j.jbusres.2021.04.070

Heredia-Calzado, M., & Duréndez, A. (2019). The influence of knowledge management and professionalization on the use of ERP systems and its effect on the competitive advantages of SMEs. In *Enterprise Information Systems* (Vol. 13, issue 9, pp. 1245–1274). Taylor and Francis Ltd. https://doi.org/10.1080/17517575.2019.1640393

Hitt, L. M., Wu, D. J., & Zhou, X. (2002). Investment in enterprise resource planning: Business impact and productivity measures. *Journal of Management Information Systems, 19*(1), 71–98. https://doi.org/10.1080/07421222.2002.11045716

Hsu, P. F., Yen, H. J. R., & Chung, J. C. (2015). Assessing ERP post-implementation success at the individual level: Revisiting the role of service quality. *Information and Management, 52*(8), 925–942. https://doi.org/10.1016/j.im.2015.06.009

Jayawickrama, U., Liu, S., & Smith, M. H. (2017). Knowledge prioritisation for ERP implementation success perspectives of clients & implementation partners in UK industries. In *Industrial management and data systems* (Vol. 117, issue 7, pp. 1521–1546). Emerald Group Publishing Ltd. https://doi.org/10.1108/IMDS-09-2016-0390

Karim, M. R., Nordin, N., Yusof, M. F., Amin, M. B., Islam, M. A., & Hassan, M. S. (2023). Does ERP implementation mediate the relationship between knowledge management and the perceived organizational performance of the healthcare sector? Evidence from a developing country. *Cogent Business and Management, 10*(3). https://doi.org/10.1080/23311975.2023.2275869

Karimi, J., Somers, T. M., & Bhattacherjee, A. (2007). The role of information systems resources in ERP capability building and business process outcomes. *Journal of Management Information Systems, 24*(2), 221–260. https://doi.org/10.2753/MIS0742-1222240209

Khalilzadeh, M., & Alikhani, A. M. (2020). The effects of PMBOK knowledge areas on the phases of ERP implementation. *Industrial Engineering & Management Systems, 19*(1), 242–253. https://doi.org/10.7232/iems.2020.19.1.242

Law, C. C. H., & Ngai, E. W. T. (2007). ERP systems adoption: An exploratory study of the organizational factors and impacts of ERP success. *Information and Management, 44*(4), 418–432. https://doi.org/10.1016/j.im.2007.03.004

Lim, K. W., & Buntine, W. (2016). Bibliographic analysis on research publications using authors, categorical labels and the citation network. *Machine Learning, 103*(2), 185–213. https://doi.org/10.1007/s10994-016-5554-z

Lutfi, A., Alshira'h, A. F., Alshirah, M. H., Al-Okaily, M., Alqudah, H., Saad, M., Ibrahim, N., & Abdelmaksoud, O. (2022). Antecedents and impacts of enterprise resource planning system adoption among Jordanian SMEs. *Sustainability (Switzerland), 14*(6). https://doi.org/10.3390/su14063508

Markus, M. L., Axline, S., Petrie, D., & Tanis, C. (2000). Learning from adopters' experiences with ERP: Problems encountered and success achieved. *Journal of Information Technology, 15*(4), 245–265. https://doi.org/10.1080/02683960010008944

McGinnis, T. C., & Huang, Z. (2007). Rethinking ERP success: A new perspective from knowledge management and continuous improvement. *Information and Management, 44*(7), 626–634. https://doi.org/10.1016/j.im.2007.05.006

Nour, M. A. (2023). The impact of ERP systems on organizational performance: The role of antecedents and moderators. *International Journal of Enterprise Information Systems (IJEIS), 19*(1), 1–29.

Ram, J., Corkindale, D., & Wu, M. L. (2013). Implementation critical success factors (CSFs) for ERP: Do they contribute to implementation success and post-implementation performance?

International Journal of Production Economics, 144(1), 157–174. https://doi.org/10.1016/j.ijpe.2013.01.032

Stratman, J. K., & Roth, A. V. (2002). Enterprise resource planning (ERP) competence constructs: Ibo-stage multi-item scale development and validation*. *Decision Sciences, 33*, 601–628.

Torres-Carrion, P. V., Gonzalez-Gonzalez, C. S., Aciar, S., & Rodriguez-Morales, G. (2018). Methodology for systematic literature review applied to engineering and education. *IEEE Global Engineering Education Conference, EDUCON, 2018-April*, 1364–1373. https://doi.org/10.1109/EDUCON.2018.8363388

Vandaie, R. (2008). The role of organizational knowledge management in successful ERP implementation projects. *Knowledge-Based Systems, 21*(8), 920–926. https://doi.org/10.1016/j.knosys.2008.04.001

Xu, L., Wang, C., Luo, X., & Shi, Z. (2006). Integrating knowledge management and ERP in enterprise information systems. *Systems Research and Behavioral Science, 23*). www.interscience.wiley.com, 147–156.

Chapter 5
Empirical Research

5.1 Introduction

In order to empirically validate the relationships between ERP systems, knowledge management (KM) and organizational performance, two different research studies were conducted, each following established research methodologies.

- **Model I: ERP acceptance model**—The first study focused on ERP adoption research, including significant element of KM alongside traditional technology adoption frameworks, which is knowledge sharing culture. With a focus on how knowledge sharing culture affect the adoption process, this study sought to analyze the various elements that motivate companies to adopt ERP systems.
- **Model II: Strategic ERP & KM synergy model**—Another research included KM practices into the analysis and looked at how ERP systems affect company performance. The purpose of this study was to clarify how important performance indicators are impacted by ERP systems when they work in combination with efficient knowledge management practices. With this strategy, the deeper impacts of ERP systems on enhancing organizational results through enhanced information distribution and strategic knowledge application were to be revealed.

5.2 Model I: ERP Acceptance Model

The first model analysed is the ERP acceptance model (presented in Fig. 5.1), which is based on the Technology Acceptance Model (TAM).

- TAM is a framework that assesses how users accept and use technology. As per this paradigm, a person's intention to use a system is determined by two main criteria: perceived usefulness and perceived ease of use.

L. Turulja et al., *Integrating ERP Systems and Knowledge Management*, Progress in IS, https://doi.org/10.1007/978-3-031-68922-2_5

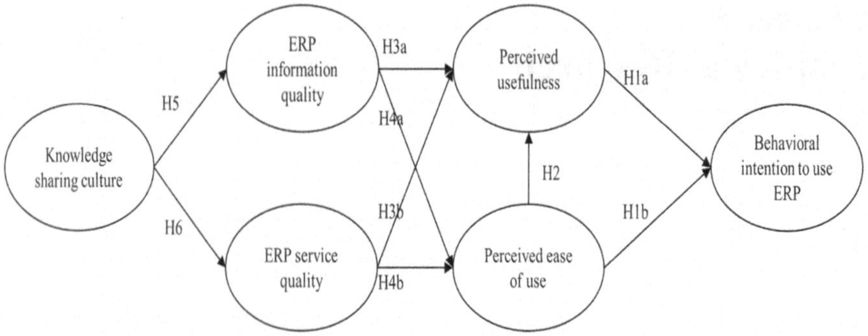

Fig. 5.1 ERP acceptance model

- The ERP acceptance model comprises two particular ERP-related variables in addition to these fundamental ones: ERP information quality and ERP service quality.
- Moreover, the model includes the knowledge sharing culture, a significant factor from the field of organizational behavior connected to knowledge management. The inclusion of this culture makes sense since it greatly enhances the knowledge management concepts. Effective information and skill distribution inside an organization is the main goal of knowledge management. An organization can learn and adjust more effectively overall if it cultivates an environment where knowledge is freely shared. Since it directly impacts the effective implementation and usage of ERP systems within organizations, this synergy between knowledge management and ERP systems emphasizes the need of including a culture of knowledge sharing into the ERP adoption model.

Hence, the proposed conceptual model includes the following variables:

1. Perceived Usefulness (PU)
2. Perceived Ease of Use (PEOU)
3. Behavioural Intentions to Use (BIUS)
4. ERP Information Quality (ERPIQ)
5. ERP Service Quality (ERPSQ)
6. Knowledge Sharing Culture (KSC)

The model is developed based on established relationships documented in existing literature. The hypothesized relationships are as follows, emphasizing how behavioural intentions for the usage of ERP are shaped:

- H1: Behavioural intentions to use ERP are positively influenced by factors defined in TAM.
  - H1a: Perceived usefulness of ERP positively influences behavioural intentions to use ERP.
  - H1b: Perceived ease of use of ERP positively influences behavioural intentions to use ERP.

- H2: Perceived ease of use of ERP influences perceived usefulness of ERP.
- H3: Perceived usefulness of ERP is impacted by specific ERP factors.
  - H2a: Perceived usefulness of ERP is positively influenced by the ERP information quality.
  - H2b: Perceived usefulness of ERP is positively influenced by the ERP service quality.
- H4: Perceived ease of use of ERP is impacted by specific ERP factors.
  - H3a: Perceived ease of use of ERP is positively influenced by the ERP information quality.
  - H3b: Perceived ease of use of ERP is positively influenced by the ERP service quality.
- H5: ERP information quality is positively influenced by a knowledge-sharing culture.
- H6: ERP service quality is positively influenced by a knowledge-sharing culture.

5.2.1 Research Hypotheses

As was covered in earlier chapters, the Technology Acceptance Model (TAM) is a theoretical framework designed to forecast and explain user behavior associated with information technology use. TAM works on the fundamental idea that behavioral intentions, which are impacted by two important perceptions, perceived usefulness (PU) and perceived ease of use (PEOU), can predict actual technology use (Davis, 1989).

- Perceived usefulness (PU): This is the degree to which an individual thinks that implementing a certain system will enhance their ability to perform at work. Perception of usefulness is the main factor predicting behavioral intention and ensuing actual system use, claims TAM. External factors including system operation, output quality, and room for job development affect this perception (Davis & Venkatesh, 1996).
- Perceived Ease of Use (PEOU): This refers to the degree to which a person believes that using a particular system would be effortless. Outside influences on this perception also include user interface design, training, and technical support. TAM contends that a technology can be seen as more useful the easier it is to use (Davis & Venkatesh, 1996).

Regarding the model's structure, TAM implies a clear connection between perceived usefulness and behavioral intention as well as between perceived ease of use and perceived usefulness. The perceived ease of use also directly affects behavioral intention. Because of these connections, a user is more inclined to form a favorable behavioral intention toward using a technology, which will probably result in actual use, if they find it helpful and easy to use.

As such, the TAM serves as the foundation for the first two hypotheses of the suggested paradigm. More precisely, these theories look into how perceived ease of use and usefulness affect behavioral intentions to use an ERP system (Davis & Venkatesh, 1996).

- *H1: Behavioural intentions to use ERP are positively influenced by factors defined in TAM.*
  - *H1a: Perceived usefulness of ERP positively influences behavioural intentions to use ERP.*
  - *H1b: Perceived ease of use of ERP positively influences behavioural intentions to use ERP.*
- *H2: Perceived ease of use of ERP influences perceived usefulness of ERP.*

The third and fourth hypotheses address how perceived usefulness and ease of use of ERP information (ERP Information Quality) and services (ERP Service Quality) are impacted. These are outside forces, or stimuli (Davis & Venkatesh, 1996). These theories have as their foundation the idea that an ERP system is more user-friendly and beneficial to its users when it provides trustworthy services and high-quality information. Users are more likely to continue using a system when they believe it to be useful and easy to use overall and to provide accurate and timely information and services (Kuo & Lee, 2009; Lin & Wu, 2002). Users' opinions of the value of technology and their level of satisfaction with it are greatly influenced by organizational and informational aspects. Kuo and Lee (2009) specifically confirmed the influence of information quality on perceived usefulness (PU) and ease of use (PEOU), finding that high-quality information favorably impacts both PU and PEOU, so promoting the success of technology adoption. They stress that user impressions of the system's usability and ease of use are enhanced by the clarity, correctness, and relevance of the information it offers. These features increase the attractiveness of the system and increase its likelihood of adoption since users believe it offers greater assistance in doing their work tasks.

- *H3: Perceived usefulness of ERP is impacted by specific ERP factors.*
  - *H2a: Perceived usefulness of ERP is positively influenced by the ERP information quality.*
  - *H2b: Perceived usefulness of ERP is positively influenced by the ERP service quality.*
- *H4: Perceived ease of use of ERP is impacted by specific ERP factors.*
  - *H3a: Perceived ease of use of ERP is positively influenced by the ERP information quality.*
  - *H3b: Perceived ease of use of ERP is positively influenced by the ERP service quality.*

Lastly, it appears from the fifth and sixth hypotheses that knowledge sharing culture improves the quality of ERP information and services. The argument goes that an organization that promotes a culture of knowledge sharing enhances the information and skill flow (Salloum et al., 2018). The ERP system output quality thus increases. Effectiveness and quality of the ERP system are increased when there is a culture of knowledge sharing to guarantee that important insights and operational knowledge are included into it. It is anticipated that this synergy between ERP quality and knowledge sharing will increase the perceived value and simplicity of use of the ERP system.

- *H5: ERP information quality is positively influenced by a knowledge-sharing culture.*
- *H6: ERP service quality is positively influenced by a knowledge-sharing culture.*

5.2.2 Research Design

Analyzing technology adoption and its outcomes in two distinct national contexts, the United States (USA) and Bosnia and Herzegovina (BiH), this study employs a quantitative research design. The main technique of data collecting is a survey, which guarantees the validity and dependability of the information gathered by using validated measurement scales for every variable.

Managers from various companies doing business in these two nations make up the study's participants. These respondents were chosen in order to offer their opinions and experiences regarding the application of technology in corporate environments. Many industries were the focus of the poll in order to record various attitudes and practices around technology adoption.

Based on well-known scales from earlier studies in the fields of management studies and technology acceptance, the survey instruments were created. These questionnaires were modified to guarantee respondents in the USA and BiH would understand them and find them contextually relevant. To suit the language choices of all participants, questionnaires are sent electronically together with instructions in both Bosnian and English.

We shall analyse the data and estimate the model using structural equation modelling (SEM), which offers a reliable statistical method to investigate connections between several variables inside our theoretical framework. Because SEM combines elements of both factor and multiple regression analyses to enable the simultaneous evaluation of several and related dependent relationships, it is especially appropriate for testing complex models.

SEM is unique among multivariate methods in that it can explicitly model constructs as latent factors—that is, factors that are deduced from several measured variables but not directly observed. The precision of the analysis is increased by this approach, which permits taking measurement error into account. Furthermore, SEM makes it possible to investigate constructs that, depending on the context of their relationship within the model, can function as both independent and dependent variables, so confirming the interdependence of the structural model (Hair et al., 2019).

Within this study, a number of structural equations expressing the connections between the dependent variable (behavioural intention to use the ERP) and the independent variables (such perceived usefulness and ease of use) will be specified and tested using SEM.

5.2.3 Research Instrument

The development of a closed-ended structured questionnaire allowed the research to cover the several aspects connected to the study. Based on current scientific work, the questionnaire was developed with few changes to fit the particular criteria of this project. Responses for the survey variables were scored on a Likert scale, which runs from 1 (strongly disagree) to 7 (strongly agree), so offering a complex spectrum for respondent comments.

Several demographic questions on the background of the respondents and the features of their businesses were also part of the questionnaire. These demographic facts will enable the analysis of the findings within several contextual models.

The last form of the questionnaire consists in particular research tools for every variable under investigation:

- Scale for Perceived usefulness (PU): Assess the extent to which users believe that using the system would improve their work performance.
- Scale for Perceived ease of use (PEOU): To determine how effortless using a system appears to users.
- Scale for Behavioural intention to use (BIUS): To measure users' intentions to engage with a system based on their perceptions of its usefulness and ease of use.
- Scale for ERP information quality (ERPIQ): To assess users' perceptions of the information provided by a system.
- Scale for ERP service quality (ERPSQ): To assess users' perceptions of the service provided by a system and IT department.
- Scale for Knowledge sharing culture (KSC): To examine the extent to which a culture of knowledge sharing is embedded in the organization.

Below are the tables in which the indicators of the measurement scales are listed.

With three items, Table 5.1 lists perceived usefulness (PU) measuring scale. A Likert scale ranging from 1 to 7 is used to evaluate these objects, so expressing degrees of agreement or disagreement. Originally from Venkatesh and Goyal (2010), the scale has been adapted to suit the framework of the study.

Featuring five items, Table 5.2 shows the measurement scale for perceived ease of use (PEOU). A Likert scale ranging from 1 to 7 is used to evaluate these objects, so expressing degrees of agreement or disagreement. Originally from (Venkatesh & Goyal, 2010), this scale has been adapted to suit the context of the research.

Table 5.1 Measurement scale for the perceived usefulness (PU)

Item code	Item
PU1	Using the ERP (enterprise resource planning or integrated information system[a]) improves my working performance
PU2	Using the ERP increases my job productivity (e.g. I do things faster, I get faster reports, I gain additional expertise, etc.)
PU3	I would find the ERP useful in my job

[a] In Bosnian/Croatian/Serbian language, ERP systems are Integrated information systems

Table 5.2 Measurement scale for the perceived ease of use (PEOU)

Item code	Item
PEOU1	My interaction with an ERP is understandable
PEOU2	The ERP that I use is flexible to work with
PEOU3	I can access all information easily
PEOU4	I can retrieve all information easily
PEOU5	I find my ERP easy to use

Table 5.3 Measurement scale for the behavioural intentions (BIUS)

Item code	Item
BIUS1	I intend to continue using the ERP
BIUS2	I predict I would continue using the ERP
BIUS3	I plan to continue using the ERP

Table 5.4 Measurement scale for the ERP information quality (ERPIQ)

Item code	Item
ERPIQ1	The content representation that I receive from my ERP is logical and clear
ERPIQ2	The knowledge or information provided by the ERP is available when I need it
ERPIQ3	The knowledge or information provided by the ERP is important and helpful for my work
ERPIQ4	The information or knowledge that I receive from the ERP is meaningful

Including three items, Table 5.3 shows behavioral intention to use (BIUS) measuring scale. On a Likert scale ranging from 1 to 7, these objects are scored; 1 denotes total disagreement and 7 total agreement. This scale has been adapted from Venkatesh and Goyal (2010) to suit the framework of our research.

Including four items, Table 5.4 shows the ERP information quality (ERPIQ) measuring scale. Using a Likert scale ranging from 1 to 7, these objects are scored as 1 denotes total disagreement and 7 total agreement. Designed with an eye toward ERP system quality, this scale has been adapted from Ouiddad et al. (2020) to fit the setting of our research.

Table 5.5 presents the measurement scale for ERP service quality (ERPSQ), which includes six items. These items are evaluated using a Likert scale ranging from 1 to 7, where 1 indicates complete disagreement and 7 indicates complete

Table 5.5 Measurement scale for the ERP service quality (ERPSQ)

Item code	Item
ERPSQ1	If I have to use new features of the ERP, written procedures on how to do it are available to me
ERPSQ2	I receive coaching or training when I use new features of the ERP
ERPSQ3	When I need to use new features (modules) of the ERP, I have a dedicated person that I communicate with
ERPSQ4	When I need to use new features (modules) of the ERP, I have support from other employees
ERPSQ5	When I need to use new features (modules) of the ERP, I receive all necessary documentation on time
ERPSQ6	When I need to use new features (modules) of the ERP, I know exactly where to find all necessary documentation or who will provide these documents to me

Table 5.6 Measurement scale for the knowedge sharing culture (KSC)

Item code	Item
KSC1	I can communicate and share knowledge with other employees
KSC2	Top management encourage us (employees) to meet and share knowledge about our job activities (e.g. team building)
KSC3	My organization has an incentive and rewards system to encourage employees to share their knowledge with others
KSC4	My organization has written (stored) policies, procedures, or guidelines to support knowledge sharing between employees
KSC5	I can use knowledge or information from the IS that is related to my job activities
KSC6	I use collaborative tools or knowledge portals to learn or to share knowledge in my organization

agreement. ERP service quality intends to measure the quality of support and resources provided to users for the effective use and adoption of new features within an ERP system, including training, documentation, and personalized assistance.

Six items aimed to evaluate different facets of knowledge sharing inside the company form the measurement scale for knowledge sharing culture (KSC), which is shown in Table 5.6. Every item gets a Likert scale rating ranging from 1 to 7; 1 denotes total disagreement and 7 denotes total agreement. Through policies, tools, and management techniques, this instrument is meant to show the degree to which the company promotes knowledge sharing among its staff members.

Apart from the mail research variables, the questionnaire comprised control variables to consider outside elements influencing the results. Among these control factors are main corporate activity and country of company registration (presented in Table 5.7). This method guarantees a thorough investigation by taking into account the possible impact of demographic and organizational aspects on ERP acceptance.

Table 5.7 Demographic variables

Item code	Item	Item measurement
Industry	Core business activity of the organization	Banking, Insurance, Finance services Consulting Services Education Institution Food and Household Government/Public Institution Health Care and Biotechnology Information Technology Infrastructure and Utilities Manufacturing, Mining, Energy Media Retail Telecommunications Tourism and Leisure Transportation
Country	Country of the company registration	Bosnia and Herzegovina, USA

5.2.4 Data Collection

This study focuses just on companies who have put ERP systems into use. The sample comprises American companies as well as Bosnia and Herzegovina (BiH) ones. These two nations were chosen to control the ERP adoption model in various settings, so offering a better knowledge of organizational environments and ERP implementation experiences.

Along with companies who have embraced ERP systems, the sample comprises end users actively engaged in the deployment process. This twin emphasis provides a whole picture of the ERP implementation scene by allowing one to get insights from both strategic decision-making and pragmatic user experience levels. This strategy guarantees enough variation of experiences and settings, so enhancing the results of the research on ERP acceptance and effects on organizational operations.

Given the emphasis of the study on companies with ERP systems, the sampling technique can be characterized as purposive. First, a search was done to find current information on businesses using ERP systems. Once these companies were found, attempts were made to get contact information for the pertinent people working for these companies directly connected to the ERP systems. This strategy guaranteed that the sample comprised informed individuals capable of giving thorough and accurate answers depending on their ERP solution experience. The goals of the research call for insight from a particular subset of the population, those personally exposed to ERP systems, thus the purposive sampling technique is suitable. Targeting respondents who fit these criteria helps the study to gather relevant information that can clarify particular research issues concerning ERP deployment and use.

The survey for this study was developed in an online format to facilitate distribution and response. Data were collected by sending an invitation to participate in the study with a link to an online survey via e-mail. This method was chosen to effectively reach the target group of respondents who are involved in ERP systems either through implementation or active use.

5.2.5 *Sample*

Using a purposive sampling technique, that is, focusing especially on companies known to have adopted ERP systems, the 161 companies that make up the study sample.

The sample reflects the several applications of ERP systems by covering several sectors, as depicted in Table 5.8. Particularly in the banking, insurance, and financial services sectors, which account for the biggest group at 17.39%, ERP systems are clearly vital in securely and effectively managing customer data, regulatory compliance, and financial transactions. Comprising 12.42% and 11.80% respectively, the media and telecommunications sectors follow them in terms of proportion. A sizable fraction of the sample (10.56%) are also related with biotechnology and healthcare. Comprising businesses that not only use but also often create ERP solutions, the information technology industry accounts for 8.07% of the sample. Together, manufacturing, mining, and energy account for 7.45% of the sample; other sectors, including education, retail, and government institutions, are also represented but in smaller numbers, so reflecting the growing reach of ERP systems outside their traditional industrial domains.

With 45.96% and 54.04% respectively, Bosnia and Herzegovina (BiH) and the United States (USA) almost balance in terms of geographic distribution of the sample. This distribution is especially interesting since it enables a comparison of ERP acceptance and efficiency in two quite different economic, cultural, and legal contexts (presented in Table 5.9).

Table 5.8 Industry distribution

Industry/Sector	%
Banking, Insurance, Finance services	17.39
Consulting Services	5.59
Education Institution	3.73
Food and Household	3.11
Government/Public Institution	4.97
Health Care and Biotechnology	10.56
Information Technology	8.07
Infrastructure and Utilities	3.11
Manufacturing, Mining, Energy	7.45
Media	11.80
Retail	4.35
Telecommunications	12.42
Tourism and Leisure	6.83
Transportation	0.62
Grand total	100.00

the rho_A values. These metrics help ensure that the constructs are consistentl represented across their respective indicators, providing a reliable basis for the analysis (Hair et al., 2014).

Validity assessment—This phase tests the validity of the model, including both convergent and discriminant validity.

Convergent validity is verified by analysing the loadings of each indicator on its respective construct, where loadings should ideally be 0.7 or higher. Additionally, the Average Variance Extracted (AVE) for each construct should be 0.5 or greater, indicating that over half of the variance observed in the indicators is due to the construct itself.

Discriminant validity is assessed to ensure that each construct is distinctly different from others in the model. This is often examined using the Fornell-Larcker criterion and the Heterotrait-Monotrait (HTMT) ratio of correlations. The Fornell-Larcker criterion requires that the square root of the AVE of each construct should be larger than its highest correlation with any other construct. Meanwhile, HTMT values should be below 0.9 (Hair et al., 2014).

e analysis was performed using the software tool SmartPLS 4.

Reliability is indicated in Table 5.11 together with convergent validity measures every measurement model construct. Ensuring the accuracy and integrity of the structs in the research model depends on these steps. Two variations of composeliability are rho_a and rho_c. Values higher than 0.7 show acceptable reliabil- values nearer or above 0.9 show very high reliability. Comparatively to the unt of variance resulting from measurement error, average variance extracted E) gauges the degree of variance captured by a construct. Desirable values e 0.5 show that the construct explains more than half of the variance of their ators. Thus, the findings confirm the reliability of the measurement model.

loreover, as shown in Table 5.12, all standardized loadings surpass the 0.7 hold, so verifying the convergent validity of the constructs within the measure- model. This shows that every indicator consistently measures its correspond- onstruct, so ensuring that the constructions accurately represent the variance ped to the fundamental conceptual concepts.

ble 5.12 presents Heterotrait-Monotrait (HTMT) ratio—while most HTMT support adequate discriminant validity between constructs, a few values,

.11 Reliability and validity statistics of constructs

	Composite reliability (rho_a)	Composite reliability (rho_c)	Average variance extracted (AVE)
	0.963	0.975	0.928
	0.897	0.925	0.755
	0.909	0.930	0.690
	0.873	0.898	0.595
	0.925	0.943	0.767
	0.926	0.951	0.867

Table 5.9 Geographic distribution of the sample

Country	%
BiH	45.96
USA	54.04
Grand total	100.00

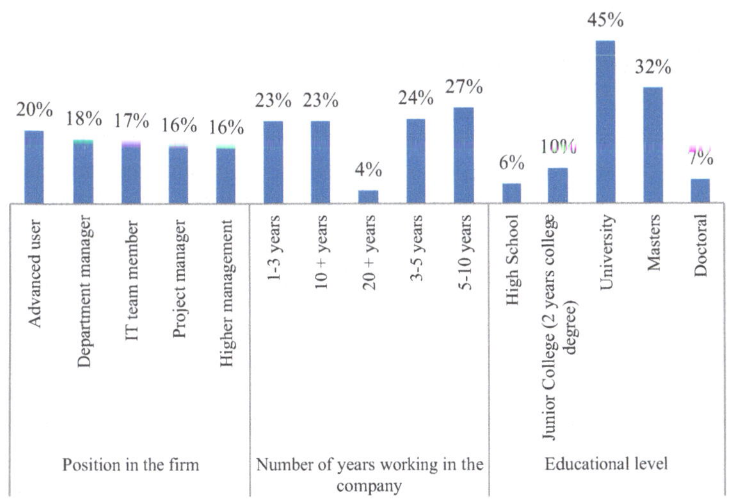

Fig. 5.2 Structure of the characteristics of respondents from the sample (selected characteristics)

Table 5.10 Provider of the main integrated information system used to perform business activities

	Frequency	Percent	Cumulative percent
SAP	9	5.59	5.59
ORACLE	31	19.25	24.84
Microsoft	47	29.19	54.04
Concur	19	11.80	65.84
Datalab Pantheon	14	8.70	74.53
5th Dimension	8	4.97	79.50
Kronos	8	4.97	84.47
POINT	3	1.86	86.34
Infosoft	2	1.24	87.58
Other	20	12.42	100.00
Total	161	100.00	

Figure 5.2 shows some characteristics of the sample's respondents. The fact that almost 45% of the respondents have a university degree shows clearly a high degree of education among the participants. About one third of respondents also have worked for the same company for 5–10 years. Twenty percent of the respondents also fit as advanced ERP system users.

Table 5.10 shows the main ERP system providers companies in the sample use to run operations. With 29.19% of the respondents using Microsoft, the data shows that this company is the most often used provider; Oracle comes second with 19.25%. Other noteworthy systems used by 11.80% and 8.70% of the sample respectively are Concur and Datalab Pantheon. POINT and Infosoft are used by just 1.86% and 1.24% of respondents on the lower end of the spectrum.

5.2.6 Data Analysis and Results

The accuracy and adequacy of the data gathered by the research must be guaranteed before statistical analysis. The procedures followed in managing any disparities, verifying the data, and getting ready for the analysis are described in this part.

- **Data entry and coding**
- To guarantee consistency throughout the dataset, answers were first meticulously coded. Putting the answers into a format appropriate for statistical analysis is the task of this step. To maintain the integrity of the study, the data were looked for any inappropriate answers or outliers, which were removed from later analyses.
- **Handling of missing values**
- The fact that every question in this survey was required reduced the possibility of missing values. Research quality can be greatly impacted by missing data since it can result in biassed findings and lower the effective sample size. The requirement that every question be answered allowed to keep the data set complete.
- **Testing the suitability of data for statistical analysis**
- In order to ensure that the collected data meet the assumptions required for robust statistical analysis, several tests were performed:
  - **Normality**
  - The normality of the variables was evaluated using the Kolmogorov-Smirnov test, which indicated deviations from normality. Since PLS-SEM will be used, this this is not problem.
  - **Multicollinearity**
  - Multicollinearity was evaluated using the variance inflation factor (VIF). no variable had a VIF greater than 10.
  - **Linearity**
  - SEM analysis assumes linear relationships between exogenous and endogenous variables. The preliminary analysis supports the assumption of linearity, making the data suitable for SEM.

Two-step method proposed by Anderson and Gerbing (1988) will be applied in data analysis. This approach guarantees a methodical analysis of the measurement model before the evaluation of the construction model, so strengthening the validity and reliability of the results.

Step 1: Estimation of the measurement model
Examining the measurement model comes first, with a focus tow both the reliability and validity of the study's used constructs. The features of the measuring scales, including their convergent validit validity, and reliability, are investigated in this stage. Establishing th cators precisely measure each construct guarantees that the cons reflect the phenomenon under investigation. This stage is crucial sin that measures are statistically robust and sufficiently represent co tions, so laying the foundation for next structural analysis.

Step 2: Estimating the structural model
The second step of the analysis, the evaluation of the structur following the validation of the measurement model. Testing the e ships among the constructions as stated in the theoretical framev comes under this phase of the research. By means of structural eq it can explain the strength and direction of these relationships, deduce underlying theory validity. This section investigates between variables using methods including path analysis inside tion modelling (SEM) framework.

The two-step approach of Anderson and Gerbing's (1988) study keeps a clear difference between measurement and str enabling the accurate interpretation of the influence of latent observed variables. By helping to reduce errors and biases resul ous assessment, this methodological separation ensures more study conclusions.

The relationships among the theoretical constructs will b research using partial least squares structural equation modeli SEM is especially appropriate for this study because of its e small to medium sample sizes, which are common in pract ments. PLS-SEM provides several benefits over conventio SEM. This makes it a great tool for examining non-normal interrelationships free from strong presumptions about the et al., 2014).

5.2.6.1 Evaluation of the Measurement Model

Using Composite Reliability, Average Variance Extract Monotrait ratio for discriminant validity, the measurement ated to guarantee validity and reliability of the constructi verify that every construct is quantified with enough acc from one another.

- **Reliability assessment**—Here the focus is on asses measurement model. This is done by examining the i construct. This typically involves checking the Comp

Table 5.9 Geographic distribution of the sample

Country	%
BiH	45.96
USA	54.04
Grand total	100.00

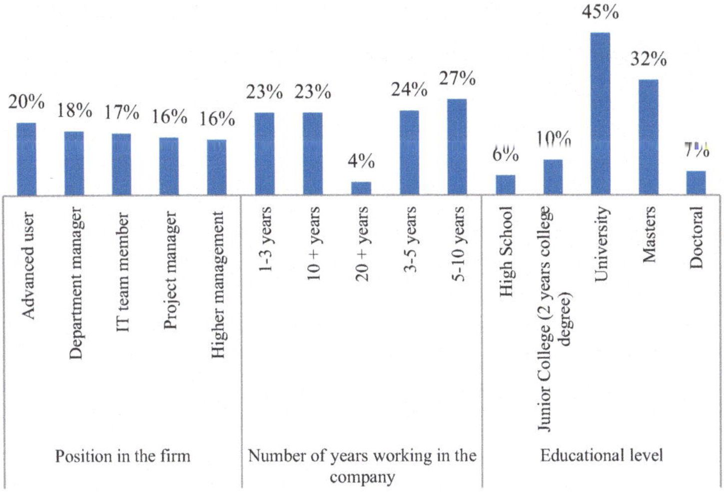

Fig. 5.2 Structure of the characteristics of respondents from the sample (selected characteristics)

Table 5.10 Provider of the main integrated information system used to perform business activities

	Frequency	Percent	Cumulative percent
SAP	9	5.59	5.59
ORACLE	31	19.25	24.84
Microsoft	47	29.19	54.04
Concur	19	11.80	65.84
Datalab Pantheon	14	8.70	74.53
5th Dimension	8	4.97	79.50
Kronos	8	4.97	84.47
POINT	3	1.86	86.34
Infosoft	2	1.24	87.58
Other	20	12.42	100.00
Total	161	100.00	

Figure 5.2 shows some characteristics of the sample's respondents. The fact that almost 45% of the respondents have a university degree shows clearly a high degree of education among the participants. About one third of respondents also have worked for the same company for 5–10 years. Twenty percent of the respondents also fit as advanced ERP system users.

Table 5.10 shows the main ERP system providers companies in the sample use to run operations. With 29.19% of the respondents using Microsoft, the data shows that this company is the most often used provider; Oracle comes second with 19.25%. Other noteworthy systems used by 11.80% and 8.70% of the sample respectively are Concur and Datalab Pantheon. POINT and Infosoft are used by just 1.86% and 1.24% of respondents on the lower end of the spectrum.

5.2.6 Data Analysis and Results

The accuracy and adequacy of the data gathered by the research must be guaranteed before statistical analysis. The procedures followed in managing any disparities, verifying the data, and getting ready for the analysis are described in this part.

- **Data entry and coding**
- To guarantee consistency throughout the dataset, answers were first meticulously coded. Putting the answers into a format appropriate for statistical analysis is the task of this step. To maintain the integrity of the study, the data were looked for any inappropriate answers or outliers, which were removed from later analyses.
- **Handling of missing values**
- The fact that every question in this survey was required reduced the possibility of missing values. Research quality can be greatly impacted by missing data since it can result in biassed findings and lower the effective sample size. The requirement that every question be answered allowed to keep the data set complete.
- **Testing the suitability of data for statistical analysis**
- In order to ensure that the collected data meet the assumptions required for robust statistical analysis, several tests were performed:
  - **Normality**
  - The normality of the variables was evaluated using the Kolmogorov-Smirnov test, which indicated deviations from normality. Since PLS-SEM will be used, this this is not problem.
  - **Multicollinearity**
  - Multicollinearity was evaluated using the variance inflation factor (VIF). no variable had a VIF greater than 10.
  - **Linearity**
  - SEM analysis assumes linear relationships between exogenous and endogenous variables. The preliminary analysis supports the assumption of linearity, making the data suitable for SEM.

Two-step method proposed by Anderson and Gerbing (1988) will be applied in data analysis. This approach guarantees a methodical analysis of the measurement model before the evaluation of the construction model, so strengthening the validity and reliability of the results.

Step 1: Estimation of the measurement model

Examining the measurement model comes first, with a focus toward verifying both the reliability and validity of the study's used constructs. The psychometric features of the measuring scales, including their convergent validity, discriminant validity, and reliability, are investigated in this stage. Establishing that suitable indicators precisely measure each construct guarantees that the constructions really reflect the phenomenon under investigation. This stage is crucial since it guarantees that measures are statistically robust and sufficiently represent conceptual definitions, so laying the foundation for next structural analysis.

Step 2: Estimating the structural model

The second step of the analysis, the evaluation of the structural model, comes following the validation of the measurement model. Testing the expected relationships among the constructions as stated in the theoretical framework of the study comes under this phase of the research. By means of structural equation modelling, it can explain the strength and direction of these relationships, so enabling us to deduce underlying theory validity. This section investigates direct interactions between variables using methods including path analysis inside a structural equation modelling (SEM) framework.

The two-step approach of Anderson and Gerbing's (1988) guarantees that the study keeps a clear difference between measurement and structural models, so enabling the accurate interpretation of the influence of latent constructions on the observed variables. By helping to reduce errors and biases resulting from simultaneous assessment, this methodological separation ensures more accurate and strong study conclusions.

The relationships among the theoretical constructs will be investigated in this research using partial least squares structural equation modeling (PLS-SEM). PLS-SEM is especially appropriate for this study because of its efficiency in managing small to medium sample sizes, which are common in practical research environments. PLS-SEM provides several benefits over conventional covariance-based SEM. This makes it a great tool for examining non-normal data and complicated interrelationships free from strong presumptions about the data distribution (Hair et al., 2014).

5.2.6.1 Evaluation of the Measurement Model

Using Composite Reliability, Average Variance Extracted, and the Heterotrait-Monotrait ratio for discriminant validity, the measurement model will first be evaluated to guarantee validity and reliability of the constructions. These measures will verify that every construct is quantified with enough accuracy and that they differ from one another.

- **Reliability assessment**—Here the focus is on assessing the reliability of the measurement model. This is done by examining the internal consistency of each construct. This typically involves checking the Composite Reliability (CR), and the rho_A values. These metrics help ensure that the constructs are consistently represented across their respective indicators, providing a reliable basis for the analysis (Hair et al., 2014).

- **Validity assessment**—This phase tests the validity of the model, including both convergent and discriminant validity.
- Convergent validity is verified by analysing the loadings of each indicator on its respective construct, where loadings should ideally be 0.7 or higher. Additionally, the Average Variance Extracted (AVE) for each construct should be 0.5 or greater, indicating that over half of the variance observed in the indicators is due to the construct itself.
- Discriminant validity is assessed to ensure that each construct is distinctly different from others in the model. This is often examined using the Fornell-Larcker criterion and the Heterotrait-Monotrait (HTMT) ratio of correlations. The Fornell-Larcker criterion requires that the square root of the AVE of each construct should be larger than its highest correlation with any other construct. Meanwhile, HTMT values should be below 0.9 (Hair et al., 2014).

The analysis was performed using the software tool SmartPLS 4.

Reliability is indicated in Table 5.11 together with convergent validity measures for every measurement model construct. Ensuring the accuracy and integrity of the constructs in the research model depends on these steps. Two variations of composite reliability are rho_a and rho_c. Values higher than 0.7 show acceptable reliability; values nearer or above 0.9 show very high reliability. Comparatively to the amount of variance resulting from measurement error, average variance extracted (AVE) gauges the degree of variance captured by a construct. Desirable values above 0.5 show that the construct explains more than half of the variance of their indicators. Thus, the findings confirm the reliability of the measurement model.

Moreover, as shown in Table 5.12, all standardized loadings surpass the 0.7 threshold, so verifying the convergent validity of the constructs within the measurement model. This shows that every indicator consistently measures its corresponding construct, so ensuring that the constructions accurately represent the variance ascribed to the fundamental conceptual concepts.

Table 5.12 presents Heterotrait-Monotrait (HTMT) ratio—while most HTMT ratios support adequate discriminant validity between constructs, a few values,

Table 5.11 Reliability and validity statistics of constructs

	Composite reliability (rho_a)	Composite reliability (rho_c)	Average variance extracted (AVE)
BIUS	0.963	0.975	0.928
ERPIQ	0.897	0.925	0.755
ERPSQ	0.909	0.930	0.690
KSC	0.873	0.898	0.595
PEOU	0.925	0.943	0.767
PU	0.926	0.951	0.867

Table 5.12 Convergent validity of constructs

	BIUS	ERPIQ	ERPSQ	KSC	PEOU	PU
BIUS1	0.960					
BIUS2	0.962					
BIUS3	0.969					
ERPIQ1		0.874				
ERPIQ2		0.869				
ERPIQ3		0.887				
ERPIQ4		0.846				
ERPSQ1			0.795			
ERPSQ2			0.850			
ERPSQ3			0.826			
ERPSQ4			0.766			
ERPSQ5			0.904			
ERPSQ6			0.835			
KSC1				0.705		
KSC2				0.827		
KSC3				0.748		
KSC4				0.773		
KSC5				0.793		
KSC6				0.779		
PEOU1					0.800	
PEOU2					0.862	
PEOU3					0.918	
PEOU4					0.906	
PEOU5					0.888	
PU1						0.951
PU2						0.911
PU3						0.931

Table 5.13 Discriminant validity—Heterotrait-Monotrait (HTMT) ratio

	BIUS	ERPIQ	ERPSQ	KSC	PEOU	PU
BIUS						
ERPIQ	0.908					
ERPSQ	0.288	0.426				
KSC	0.309	0.451	0.826			
PEOU	0.663	0.858	0.417	0.430		
PU	0.913	0.840	0.253	0.318	0.695	

particularly between BIUS and both ERPIQ and PU, approach the usual threshold of 0.90 (Table 5.13).

Although some of the Heterotrait-Monotrait (HTMT) ratios approach or reach the threshold, implying a possible overlap among some constructions, the Fornell-Larcker criterion offers more proof to support discriminant validity across all

Table 5.14 Discriminant validity—Fornell-Larcker criterion

	BIUS	ERPIQ	ERPSQ	KSC	PEOU	PU
BIUS	0.964					
ERPIQ	0.841	0.869				
ERPSQ	0.270	0.391	0.830			
KSC	0.312	0.432	0.749	0.772		
PEOU	0.625	0.787	0.383	0.413	0.876	
PU	0.861	0.764	0.233	0.316	0.642	0.931

Note: Square root of AVE is on diagonal, and correlations are below

constructs. Comparing the square root of the Average Variance Extracted (AVE) for every construct against the correlations with other constructions helps to find this criterion especially robust.

Every construct shares more variance with its indicators according to the Fornell-Larcker criterion than with those of any other construct. This robustness given by the Fornell-Larcker criterion helps to allay concerns about the possible absence of discriminant validity recommended by the HTMT ratios. It proves that every construct is really different and captures special features of the data, which is necessary for the reliability and validity of the overall structure of the model. In Table 5.14, diagonal values are square root of AVE, while correlations are below.

Following the validation of the measurement model, the structural model was examined. This involves assessing the relationships between the constructs to understand the causal relationships within the hypothesized model. Key metrics such as path coefficients, R-squared (R^2), effect sizes (f^2), and predictive relevance (Q^2) were evaluated to determine the strength and significance of these relationships.

5.2.6.2 Evaluation of the Structural Model

The structural model was evaluated using a set of methodical procedures meant to confirm the relationships among the constructs of the theoretical framework. These steps include (Hair et al., 2014):

- Assessing collinearity issues (VIF)—Evaluating a structural model in PLS-SEM starts with the collinearity assessment, which guarantees that the tested relationships are free from too strong influence of multicollinearity among predictors. This fundamental step helps the validity and reliability of the later analyses and conclusions of the model.
- Magnitude and significance of path coefficients—Path coefficients were investigated in order to evaluate the strength and significance of relationships between constructs. Bootstrapping techniques were used to test these coefficients for statistical significance, so illuminating expected causal links within the model.

- Coefficients of determination (R^2)—R^2 values were calculated for each endogenous construct within the model. This measure shows the proportion of variance in the dependent variables that can be predicted from the independent variables. Strong predictive models are indicated by higher R^2 values, which indicate that the model explains a noteworthy amount of the variance in the dependent variables.
- f^2 effect sizes—Effect sizes (f^2) were calculated to assess the influence of each predictor construct on the R^2 value of the dependent constructs. With values of 0.02, 0.15, and 0.35 indicating small, medium, and large effects respectively, this measure helps determine the relative influence of every predictor. It clarifies the pragmatic importance of the examined relationships.
- Predictive relevance (Q^2)—This indicator gauges whether the model can forecast data points omitted during the parameter estimate process. A Q^2 value higher than zero for a given endogenous construct denotes that the model is predictive relevant for that construct.

The ERP acceptance model, presented in Fig. 5.2, grounded in the Technology Acceptance Model (TAM) framework offers a comprehensive overview of how various elements contribute to the adoption and effective use of ERP systems within organizations. Theoretically, the model emphasizes the importance of both perceived usefulness and perceived ease of use as primary drivers for user acceptance and intention to engage with technology, which is consistent with core TAM principles (Fig. 5.3).

Results of hypotheses testing are presented in Table 5.15. A it can be seen, out of nine (sub)hypotheses, 6 are supported in this study. Supported by the data ($\beta = 0.782$; $t = 12.481$, $p < 0.01$), the first hypothesis (H1a) put a strong positive influence of perceived usefulness (PU) on behavioural intentions to use ERP (BIUS). This result emphasizes the part that perceived usefulness plays in motivating users to interact with the ERP system. By contrast, H1b investigated how perceived ease of use (PEOU) affected BIUS and found a weaker but statistically significant link ($\beta = 0.123$; $t = 1.763$, $p = 0.1$). This suggests that, although ease of use does affect behavioural intentions, its impact is rather less than that of perceived usefulness.

H2 posing that PEOU would significantly impact PU did not find support in the data ($\beta = 0.126$; $t = 1.123$, $p = 0.262$), implying that ease of use may not be a strong predictor of how useful users view the ERP system to be. The characteristics of the respondents could provide one reasonable explanation for this observation. As the sample's description outlines, nearly all of the respondents are advanced ERP system users. Based on their experience and familiarity with ERP systems, advanced users could have developed a degree of knowledge that renders them less sensitive to changes in service quality. These users could give information's quality and functionality top priority over service since they can effectively navigate the system without much help needed. When using ERP systems, advanced users typically have better problem-solving abilities; their expectations may be more on the system's capabilities and the quality of information it provides than on support services.

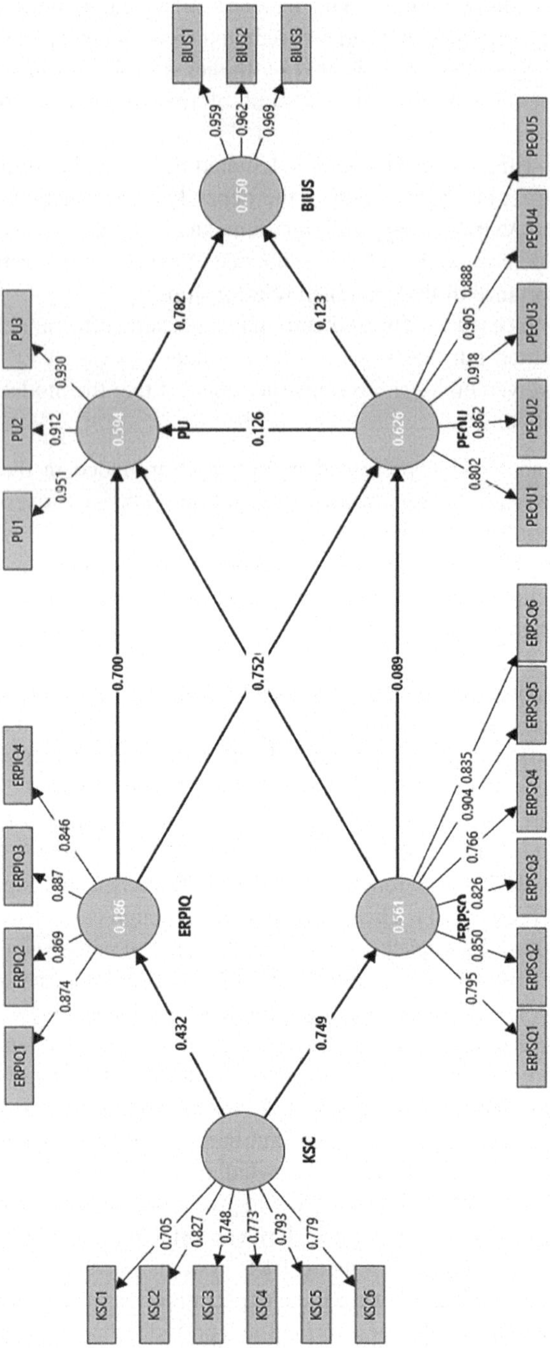

Fig. 5.3 ERP acceptance model

Table 5.15 Structural model evaluation

		Original sample (O)	Sample mean (M)	Standard deviation (STDEV)	T statistics (|O/STDEV|)	P values	R^2
H1a	PU → BIUS	0.782	0.781	0.063	12.481	0.000	0.746
H1b	PEOU → BIUS	0.123	0.124	0.070	1.763	0.078	0.746
H2	PEOU → PU	0.126	0.122	0.112	1.123	0.262	0.587
H3a	ERPIQ → PU	0.700	0.706	0.103	6.770	0.000	0.587
H3b	ERPSQ → PU	−0.089	−0.094	0.063	1.409	0.159	0.587
H4a	ERPIQ → PEOU	0.752	0.757	0.047	15.870	0.000	0.621
H4b	ERPSQ → PEOU	0.089	0.085	0.069	1.290	0.197	0.621
H5	KSC → ERPIQ	0.432	0.437	0.079	5.455	0.000	0.181
H6	KSC → ERPSQ	0.749	0.755	0.041	18.413	0.000	0.559

In testing the effects of ERP information quality (ERPIQ) on perceived usefulness, hypothesis H3a was strongly supported ($\beta = 0.700$; $t = 6.770$, $p < 0.01$), indicating that high-quality information significantly enhances users' perceptions of ERP usefulness. ERP service quality (ERPSQ) did, however, not only lack support but also show a modest negative association ($\beta = -0.089$; $t = 1.409$, $p = 0.159$), suggesting that either service quality could not match user expectations of usefulness or could be perceived as pressure.

Further analyses revealed a strong positive effect of ERP Information quality on perceived ease of use (H4a) ($\beta = 0.752$; $t = 15.870$, $p < 0.01$), demonstrating that information quality greatly facilitates ease of use. ERP service quality had a negligible and non-significant effect on perceived ease of use (H4b), however ($\beta = 0.089$; $t = 1.290$, $p = 0.197$).

Finally, Knowledge Sharing Culture (KSC) was hypothesised to influence ERP Service Quality (H6) and ERP Information Quality (H5). Both hypotheses were validated (H5: $\beta = 0.432$; $t = 5.455$, $p = 0.01$; H6: $\beta = 0.749$; $t = 18.414$, $p = 0.01$), so demonstrating that a culture encouraging knowledge sharing greatly improves the quality of both ERP information and services.

The R^2 values obtained from the structural model offer new perspectives on the extent of the variance in each endogenous variable explained by corresponding exogenous predictors. The strong R^2 value of 0.746 for the relationships involving behavioural intentions to use system (BIUS) indicates that perceived usefulness (PU) and perceived ease of use (PEOU) significantly account for about 74.6% of the variance in BIUS. Given their great impact on user intentions, improvements in system usability and ease of use could thus clearly increase user adoption rates. With regard to perceived usefulness (PU), the R^2 value of 0.587 indicates that variables including PEOU, ERP information quality (ERPIQ), and ERP service quality (ERPSQ) account for over half of the variance. This level emphasizes the relevance of these elements and implies that other factors could also help to explain PU, particularly considering the rather smaller influence of ERPSQ. Likewise, the R^2 value of 0.621 for perceived ease of use (PEOU) shows that a major portion of the variance in ERP information and services explains. With room for further considerations in next studies, this value indicates a strong reliance of user ease of use perceptions on the informational and service quality of ERP systems. On the other hand, the modest R^2 value of 0.181 shows that although knowledge sharing culture (KSC) affects ERP information quality (ERPIQ), a great amount of the variance remains inexplicable by this factor alone. This implies that other significant factors influencing information quality outside of KSC exist. Furthermore, showing a more impact is the examination of KSC's effect on ERP service quality (ERPSQ) using a R^2 of 0.559. This implies that KSC explains almost half of the variance in ERPSQ, suggesting a clear influence.

Table 5.16 shows, for every relationship in the structural model, the f^2 effect sizes. When all other variables are kept constant, effect sizes, f^2, helps one understand the change in one variable's impact on another. Their computation is based on the comparison of the variance explained in the dependent variable both with and without a predictor variable. Effect sizes of 0.02, 0.15, and 0.35 respectively indicate small, medium, and large impacts, respectively, according to (Cohen, 1988).

The computed f^2 effect sizes for the structural model provide results on the impact of various predictors on their corresponding outputs. Especially, the strong influence of perceived usefulness (PU) on behavioural intentions to use the system (BIUS) and ERP information quality (ERP) on perceived usefulness (PU) and perceived ease of use (PEOU) underlines the important part these constructs play in forming user perspective and behaviour. Particularly, the f^2 of 1.435 for the influence of PU on BIUS shows a noteworthy effect, implying that changes in users' perceptions of the system's usefulness could considerably raise their intentions to use it. Likewise, the significant impact of ERPIQ on PU ($f^2 = 1.281$) and on PEOU ($f^2 = 0.448$) emphasizes the need of information quality in the whole user experience of system usefulness and ease of use. These results imply that more positive user engagement and satisfaction results may follow from initiatives to enhance information quality and perceived usefulness in ERP systems.

Table 5.16 f^2 effect sizes

	BIUS	ERPIQ	ERPSQ	KSC	PEOU	PU
BIUS						
ERPIQ					1.281	0.448
ERPSQ					0.018	0.016
KSC		0.229	1.280			
PEOU	0.035					0.015
PU	1.435					

Table 5.17 Predictive relevance (Q^2)

	Q^2	RMSE	MAE
BIUS	0.083	0.974	0.81
ERPIQ	0.165	0.933	0.733
ERPSQ	0.546	0.683	0.476
PEOU	0.157	0.935	0.75
PU	0.085	0.975	0.831

The small effects found for ERP service quality on perceived usefulness (PU) and perceived ease of use (PEOU) imply that service quality may not be a main determinant in shaping user perceptions within this specific study setting. This result calls for more research to explain why service quality seems to have a limited influence, particularly considering that in many models service quality is regarded as a fundamental component of customer satisfaction and system acceptance.

The results presented in Table 5.17 on predictive relevance (Q^2), root mean square error (RMSE), and mean absolute error (MAE) provide insightful analysis of the structural model's performance inside the PLS-SEM paradigm. These metrics assess how well the model can predict and explain each endogenous construct.

Starting with Q^2 values, positive values are observed in every construct, so indicating predictive relevance. For example, the Q^2 value for BIUS at 0.083, although modest, confirms that the model possesses some predictive power for behavioural intentions to use the system. Analogously, the Q^2 values for ERPIQ and PEOU are 0.165 and 0.157, respectively, so verifying that the model is rather successful in predicting these features of ERP system usage from the observed data.

Particularly noteworthy is the Q2 value for ERPSQ, which at 0.546 shows great predictive relevance and suggests that the model is quite capable of predicting characteristics associated with ERP service quality. Lower RMSE and MAE values (0.683 and 0.476 respectively) for ERPSQ, which indicates a closer fit to real data and less error relative to other constructs, balance this.

On the other hand, like BIUS, perceived usefulness (PU) also shows a smaller Q^2 value of 0.085, implying a modest but positive predictive power. Though still within a range that supports some degree of predictive relevance, the RMSE and MAE for PU are somewhat higher, at 0.975 and 0.831 respectively, implying larger deviations from observed values.

Figure 5.4 presents results of evaluation of ERP acceptance model with control variables, while detailed results are presented in Table 5.18. To find whether two control variables, industry and country, BiH, USA, could affect the results differently, the model was reassessed including two such variables. According to the results of this additional investigation, adding these control variables had no effect on the overall model's results. More specifically, behavioural intentions to use system (BIUS) showed no observed influence of either industry type or country. This consistency suggests that the determinants of ERP acceptance explored in the model are robust across different industry sectors and geographical locations. It also reinforces the notion that the core factors influencing ERP adoption and usage are

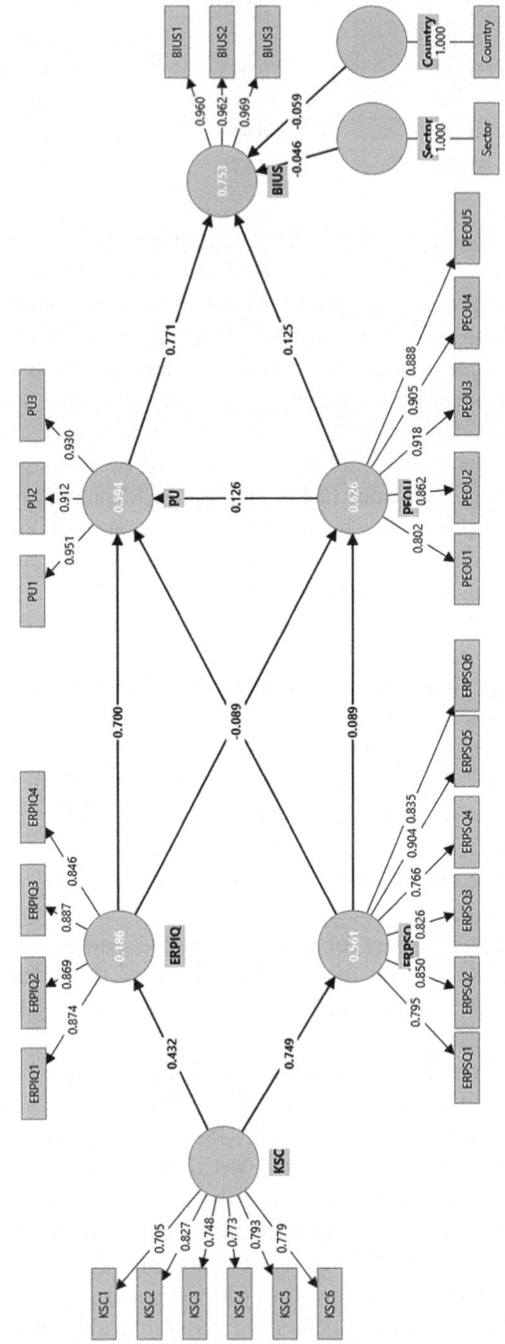

Fig. 5.4 ERP acceptance model with control variables

Table 5.18 Structural model with control variables evaluation

	Original sample (O)	Sample mean (M)	Standard deviation (STDEV)	T statistics (|O/STDEV|)	P values
PU → BIUS	0.771	0.772	0.063	12.171	0.000
PEOU → BIUS	0.125	0.126	0.068	1.841	0.066
PEOU → PU	0.126	0.122	0.112	1.123	0.262
ERPIQ → PU	0.700	0.706	0.103	6.770	0.000
ERPSQ → PU	−0.089	−0.094	0.063	1.409	0.159
ERPIQ → PEOU	0.752	0.757	0.047	15.870	0.000
ERPSQ → PEOU	0.089	0.085	0.069	1.290	0.197
KSC → ERPIQ	0.432	0.437	0.079	5.455	0.000
KSC → ERPSQ	0.749	0.755	0.041	18.413	0.000
Sector → BIUS	−0.046	−0.043	0.037	1.226	0.220
Country → BIUS	−0.059	−0.051	0.083	0.706	0.480

largely universal, transcending specific industry and national contexts. This result gives the model more validity and supports its applicability and relevance in many environments without the need of change depending on industry type or geographical location.

5.2.6.3 Discussion of the Results

By combining particular ERP-related quality factors and organizational culture, the ERP acceptance model expands conventional TAM and offers a more complete theoretical framework for understanding ERP adoption. It emphasizes the several dimensions of technology acceptance in which technical, human, and organizational aspects interact. Explaining the dynamics of ERP systems, which are complicated and deeply ingrained in the user's workflow and organizational processes, relies especially on this comprehensive approach. By tying these views to quality and cultural elements inside the company, the model emphasizes the relevance of perceived usefulness and ease of use and enriches knowledge.

Using a TAM-based ERP acceptance model, this study investigated several hypotheses regarding the elements affecting ERP adoption and use. The results help one to grasp how perceived usefulness and ease of use, together with ERP system quality dimensions and knowledge sharing culture influence user behavior and system acceptance.

The acceptance of the hypothesis that perceived usefulness (PU) significantly influences behavioral intentions to use ERP emphasizes the important part of perceived benefits in technology acceptance. This outcome is consistent with earlier research including those by Erasmus et al. (2015) and Gumussoy et al. (2007), which repeatedly showed the important influence of perceived usefulness on ERP system acceptance in many sectors. The great link between PU and behavioral intentions emphasizes the need of stressing the functional advantages and performance improvements given by ERP systems to promote user acceptance.

In contrast, findings regarding perceived ease of use (PEOU) and its impact on behavioral intentions are more mixed. While PEOU is theoretically posited as a key determinant of technology acceptance, its direct influence on PU is not supported in this model. This reflects a more complex reality captured in different studies where the impact of PEOU varies. For example, Shivers-Blackwell and Charles (2006) and Ike Wahyuning et al. (2019) found minimal or no impact of PEOU in different settings. This suggests that the importance of ease of use may depend on specific user contexts or system types, highlighting the need for targeted user experience strategies in ERP system implementation.

The model further examines the influence of ERP information quality (ERPIQ) and ERP service quality (ERPSQ) on PU and PEOU. Here, information quality greatly improves perceived usefulness and ease of use, so reflecting results from earlier studies such as those of Abugabah et al. (2015) and Kuo and Lee (2009). These findings support the need of timely, relevant, high-quality data in ERP systems to increase user perceptions and acceptance.

Furthermore, underlined by the positive influence of knowledge sharing culture (KSC) on information and service quality is the part organizational environment plays in ERP success. Studies such as those by Imam and Zaheer (2021) confirm that this result is in line with literature implying that organizations encouraging open communication and knowledge sharing may considerably improve system quality and user satisfaction.

5.2.6.4 Research Limitations

When considering the limitations of this ERP acceptance model applying the Technology Acceptance Model (TAM), several important limitations are apparent. Dealing with these limitations will help to place the results in context and offer a framework for next investigations that will build on the basis this work offers.

The sampling procedure was not random, which could introduce selection bias into the study. Non-random sampling reduces the generalizability of the results since participants might not fairly reflect the larger ERP user population. This kind of sampling can compromise external validity, so making it challenging to generalize the results of the study to many diverse companies or settings.

The study had to be carried out with a smaller sample size than is often advised for structural equation modelling (SEM). SEM calls for a bigger sample size to guarantee model estimate stability and reliability. A smaller sample size can result in less exact estimations and possibly overfitting models, so undermining confidence in the conclusions of the study. To overcome this limitation, PLS-SEM method was applied.

Future research could focus on using random sampling methods to make the sample more representative in order to get around these problems. Adding more companies from different industries and maybe comparing differences between regions in different countries could help the study go deeper. Also, making the sample size bigger might help get more reliable and applicable results.

5.2.7 Conclusion

This research proposes an ERP acceptance model consisting of six hypotheses that deal with the integration of fundamental constructs from the technology acceptance model (TAM) with specific attributes of the ERP system, taking into account the antecedent role of knowledge sharing culture. The initial hypothesis investigates how perceived usefulness and ease of use of an ERP system shape behavioral intentions to use it, fundamental elements of the TAM that define user acceptance and consequent use. More specifically, the first hypothesis investigates whether users' perceptions of the system's usefulness and ease of use significantly impact their intentions to interact with an ERP system. This implies that users' drive to use the ERP system rises when they discover it beneficial for enhancing their performance of their work. Furthermore, under consideration in this hypothesis is whether the usefulness and ease of use of an ERP system motivate users to incorporate it into their regular activities.

The model then investigates how apparent usefulness of an ERP system might be influenced by perceived ease of use. This reflects the understanding that the ease of use a system can raise the user's perception of its usefulness, so rendering the system not only simpler but also more valuable in the perspective of the user. Beyond the fundamental TAM constructions, i.e., including stimuli that are also mentioned in TAM, i.e., include particular ERP characteristics, such information and service quality, and how they influence perceived usefulness and ease of use? The study contends that while better service quality could support these perceptions, so enhancing the general system acceptance, a higher quality of information given by an ERP system could make the system seem more useful and easier to use.

Furthermore, the hypotheses cover organizational elements, looking at how the knowledge-sharing culture of a company influences the quality of information output produces by an ERP system. This method acknowledges that the success and efficiency of an ERP system can be greatly influenced by the social and cultural surroundings of a company, so indirectly affecting user acceptance and perception.

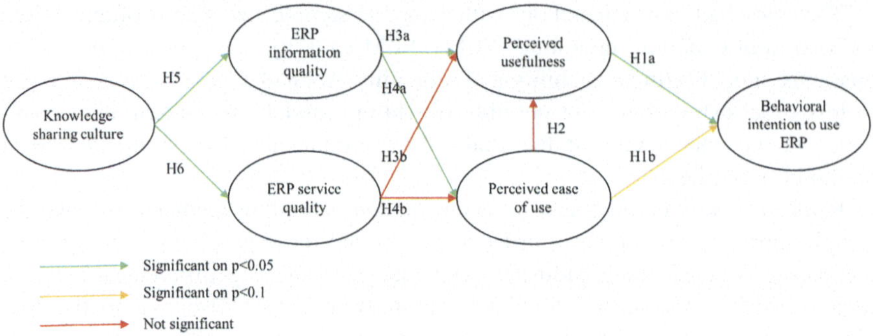

Fig. 5.5 ERP acceptance model conclusion

The proposed ERP acceptance model, as presented in Fig. 5.5, reveals results on factors that significantly impact the adoption and efficient use of ERP systems in corporate environments. These findings highlight the interaction between users' perceptions of the usefulness and ease of use of an ERP system as well as the impact of ERP-specific characteristics such as information and service quality.

Beginning with the fundamental ideas of the technology acceptance model, the results reveal a clear effect of perceived usefulness on users' intentions to use an ERP system. This implies that users' likelihood of using the system rises significantly when they perceive ERP as helpful, particularly in terms of enhancing work performance or efficiency. This feature of the model highlights the need of explaining to possible users the concrete advantages of the ERP system to raise the adoption rate.

Conversely, although positive, the impact of perceived ease of use on behavioural intentions is less clear. This suggests that, although crucial, simplicity of use might not be as decisive of a factor influencing user acceptance as the real value of the system. Practically speaking, this would mean that, even if efforts to simplify and streamline the user interface are important, they should not eclipse enhancements to the main functionalities and advantages of an ERP system. It is crucial to underline, though, that maybe this outcome was obtained since the respondents were already more advanced system users. In this sense, advanced users' knowledge and experience with an ERP system could cause them to give functional depth and customizing choices top priority over simplicity of use. For companies using ERP systems, then, knowing the particular needs and use patterns of their user base is absolutely vital. Customizing support and training tools to enable consumers to leverage advanced capabilities will raise user satisfaction and general system effectiveness. This approach also underlines the need of continuous user education and engagement strategies to guarantee that users completely appreciate and use the capabilities of the system to their full potential, so optimizing the investment in ERP technology.

Further investigation of the relationships inside the model reveals that ERP information quality has quite strong influence on perceived usefulness, meaning that accurate, high-quality information from the ERP system increases its usefulness perception among users. This result emphasizes the need of ERP systems to offer data management and processing capacity able to consistently support decision-making procedures.

Conversely, the relationship between ERP service quality and perceived usefulness shows a small negative influence. Perhaps the reason for this result is that users who are more self-sufficient or experienced with the ERP system perceive the need of extensive support services as an indication of system complexity or inefficiency, since ERP service refers to the availability of support and instructions for using the ERP. Such users may view the great degree of support needed not as an advantage but as a drawback, suggesting that the system is not well-integrated into their daily workflow or intuitive. This impression can result in a negative assessment of the general value of the ERP, particularly if users believe they are wasting too much time learning how to use system capabilities or troubleshooting.

Furthermore, the model looks at how the information and ERP system service quality is improved by the knowledge exchange culture inside companies. This implies that environments that support open communication and information sharing enhance the efficiency of ERP systems, so raising their general quality and hence their acceptance. The positive impacts of knowledge sharing culture on ERP information and service quality underline the part of organizational culture in technology adoption and imply that encouraging a cooperative and motivating work environment can greatly increase the effectiveness of technology implementations.

5.3 Model II: Strategic ERP & KM Synergy Model

This model seeks to empirically test how ERP (Enterprise Resource Planning) and KM (Knowledge Management) synergy affects the company performance. The variables of interest thus are ERP, KM, and organizational performance.

Enterprise resource planning (ERP) is, as already explained, a complete software package meant to oversee and combine transactional and operational systems inside a company. ERP systems seek to simplify operations by automating these tasks and centralizing data, so enhancing efficiency and supporting decision-making all around the company.

Dimensions of ERP quality (Ouiddad et al., 2020):

- **Information quality**—This refers to the accuracy, timeliness, relevance and understandability of the data provided by the ERP system. High quality information ensures that the data is useful and reliable for decision making.
- **System quality**—System quality assesses the technical performance of an ERP system, including its usability, adaptability, response time, and reliability. The high-quality system is easy to use and robust, minimizing downtime and technical issues that can affect productivity.

- **Service quality**—This dimension measures the support and services provided to ERP system users, including technical support and user training. Effective quality of service is key to maintaining system efficiency and ensuring user satisfaction.

On the other hand, **knowledge management (KM)** is a systematic method whereby knowledge assets of a company are managed to satisfy strategic needs and produce value. It concerns the acquisition, dissemination, application, and organization of knowledge and information inside a company.

The dimensions of KM include (Tan & Wong, 2015):

- **Knowledge acquisition**—Acquiring knowledge is the process of gathering, capturing, or obtaining knowledge from many sources. Learning from professionals, database searches, or outside sources including consultants, partners, or industry practices can all be part of this process.
- **Knowledge creation and generation**—Knowledge generation and creation is the process by which fresh ideas, insights, or innovations are produced inside an organization. Through cooperation and interaction, it often transforms tacit knowledge—personal knowledge—into explicit knowledge—documented procedures.
- **Knowledge utilization and application**—Knowledge use and application is about properly applying acquired and produced knowledge to enhance corporate processes, products, or services. It guarantees that operational effectiveness and strategic goals are reached using the knowledge.
- **Knowledge storing and updating**—Documentation, storage, and maintenance of knowledge in databases, document management systems, or other digital repositories constitute part of knowledge storing and updating. It also includes updating existing knowledge to keep it relevant as the business environment and technologies evolve.
- **Knowledge sharing and transferring**—Through training courses, seminars, cooperative tools, or intranets, this process concentrates on spreading knowledge throughout the company so that every staff member has access to required knowledge when needed.
- **Knowledge protection**—Deals with securing sensitive information from unauthorized access, theft, or leakage. It involves setting up security protocols, rights management, and ensuring compliance with legal and regulatory requirements related to intellectual property and data privacy.

The aim of this model is to assess the synergetic effect of ERP and KM on organizational performance. For organizational performance, financial performance indicators are the primary metrics considered.

A firm's capacity to generate income from its assets resulting from its main operations is referred to as its **financial performance**. Evaluating a company's efficiency in turning investment in its operations into net income depends mostly on this indicator. Many times, financial performance is expressed using several financial indicators including profitability, return on assets, cost savings, market share, return on equity, and income expansion (Chen et al., 2009). These indicators provide a quantitative tool for evaluating the economic results of the company's business activities.

The conceptual model is meant to evaluate how ERP and KM together affect organizational performance. This model suggests the following variables and combines known relationships documented in existing literature:

- ERP (enterprise resource planning)
- KM (knowledge management)
- FP (organizational/business performance)

The model hypothesizes specific relationships highlighting the synergistic influence of ERP and KM on organizational performance and it is presented in Fig. 5.6:

- H1: ERP influences KM.
  - H1a: ERP influences Knowledge acquisition
  - H1b: ERP influences Knowledge creation and generation
  - H1c: ERP influences Knowledge utilization and application

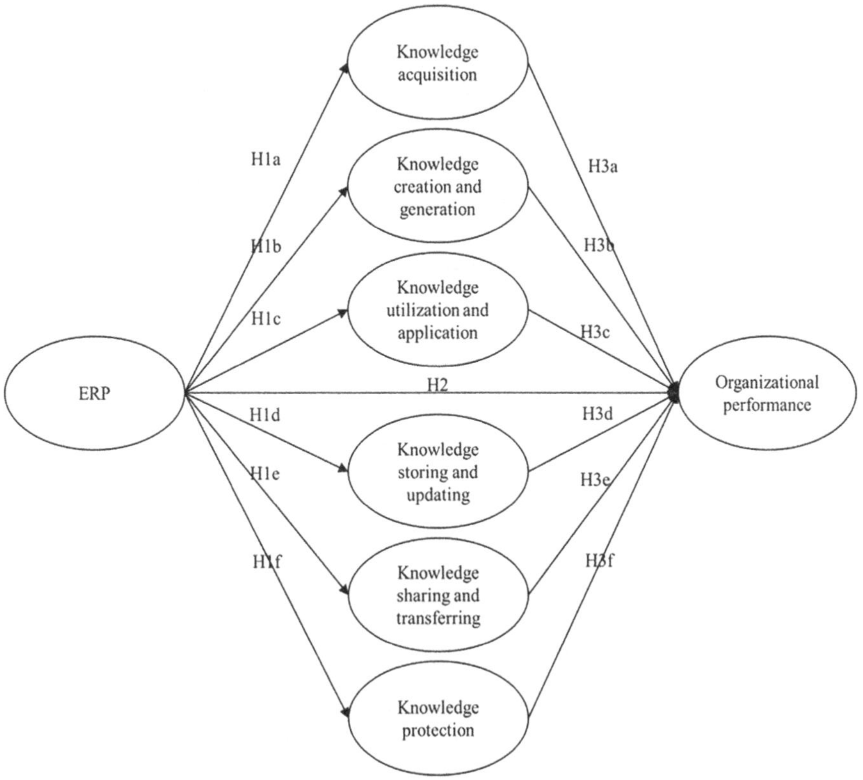

Fig. 5.6 Strategic ERP & KM synergy model

  - H1d: ERP influences Knowledge storing and updating
  - H1e: ERP influences Knowledge sharing and transferring
  - H1f: ERP influences Knowledge protection

- H2: ERP directly influences organizational performance.
- H3: KM influences organizational performance.
  - H3a: Knowledge acquisition influences organizational performance.
  - H3b: Knowledge creation and generation influences organizational performance.
  - H3c: Knowledge utilization and application influences organizational performance.
  - H3d: Knowledge storing and updating influences organizational performance.
  - H3e: Knowledge Sharing and Transferring influences organizational performance.
  - H3f: Knowledge protection influences organizational performance.
- H4: KM mediates the relationship between ERP and organizational performance.
  - H4a: Knowledge acquisition mediates the relationship between ERP and organizational performance.
  - H4b: Knowledge creation and generation mediates the relationship between ERP and organizational performance.
  - H4c: Knowledge utilization and application mediates the relationship between ERP and organizational performance.
  - H4d: Knowledge storing and updating mediates the relationship between ERP and organizational performance.
  - H4e: Knowledge sharing and transferring mediates the relationship between ERP and organizational performance.
  - H4f: Knowledge protection mediates the relationship between ERP and organizational performance.

5.3.1 Research Hypotheses

The model is grounded in the Dynamic Capability View (DCV), which revises the traditional resource-based view by introducing a dynamic perspective on resource management. DCV argues that the advantage resides not in static resources but in a company's agility in modifying and improving these resources in response to evolving market conditions (Helfat & Peteraf, 2009). Dynamic capabilities are thus described as the firm's ability to strategically manipulate its resource base to meet specific objectives (Chen & Fong, 2012).

This theory is further elaborated by scholars who underline that the fast-paced changes characteristic of today's economy urge companies to use their capabilities more effectively and quickly than rivals in order to retain competitive advantage and ensure sustainability (Teece et al., 1997). Therefore, companies have to be always changing, scale and reorganize their resources to create dynamic capabilities that are essential to maintain a competitive position and reach business success in the current economic environment.

First hypotheses in the model clarify the relationship between ERP and KM, hence also between ERP and all dimensions of KM. To stay competitive in the competitive corporate environment of nowadays, companies are realizing more and more the need of including and improving their own internal business processes. This integration and optimization helps minimize costs, improve product and service quality, and increase customer satisfaction (Metaxiotis, 2009). Moreover, leveraging and updating organizational knowledge is critical to maintaining competitive advantage and avoiding knowledge loss. Reaching these goals requires ERP and knowledge management working together. ERP systems help different business processes to be integrated, so improving operational effectiveness and lowering the production activity time needed. Companies of all sizes and industries strive to maximize output and minimize expenses and it depends on this simplified efficiency.

At the same time, KM focuses on the effective use of the organization's knowledge to improve competitive advantages. KM practice involves the creation, retention, transfer and application of knowledge, ensuring that valuable insights and innovations derived from internal and external data are used effectively (Metaxiotis, 2009). Although they contribute less to production processes, ERP systems help businesses gain a competitive advantage by producing, sharing and managing key information. This information leads to cost reduction, improved resource control and improved quality of decisions. On the other hand, knowledge management emphasizes increasing competitive advantage by applying the organization's knowledge resources in a more efficient manner. It emphasizes flexibility and innovation, as opposed to the efficiency orientation of ERP.

Sedera and Gable (2010), who investigated the relationship between knowledge management (KM) competence and ERP performance, found that there was a positive and significant relationship between the two constructs. Elaborating on this synergy, they discussed how ERP success is significantly influenced by knowledge management (KM) competence, in areas such as knowledge creation and retention, which in turn reinforces the view that ERP provides the infrastructure that supports knowledge management activities. In addition, Acar et al. (2017) conducted research on the relationship between ERP and KM and found that ERP systems facilitate the implementation of KM practices.

- *H1: ERP influences KM.*
  - *H1a: ERP influences Knowledge acquisition*
  - *H1b: ERP influences Knowledge creation and generation*
  - *H1c: ERP influences Knowledge utilization and application*
  - *H1d: ERP influences Knowledge storing and updating*
  - *H1e: ERP influences Knowledge sharing and transferring*
  - *H1f: ERP influences Knowledge protection*

The second hypothesis asserts that ERP systems directly improve the performance of organizations by helping to simplify and integrate essential business processes, which in turn improves the organization's decision-making capacity and increases efficiency. ERP systems free up the time employees would spend on manual data entry and processing because they automate routine tasks. A task that once took hours to complete can now be completed in minutes thanks to this automation, which also helps reduce errors and increase efficiency. According to Acar et al. (2017), such efficiency speeds up operations, and consequently reduces operating costs by reducing the amount of manual labor required to perform those operations.

- *H2: ERP directly influences organizational performance.*

Following Acar et al. (2017), the third hypothesis concerning the impact of knowledge management on organizational performance is based on the assumption that it is necessary to effectively manage and use knowledge in order to improve decision-making, encourage innovation and maintain competitive advantage. The collection, organization and analysis of information is facilitated by knowledge management systems, which transform raw data into actionable information and knowledge. With knowledge that is comprehensive and readily available, managers and employees are able to make decisions that are well-informed and fast, enabling them to effectively respond to both opportunities and challenges in the business world. This informed decision-making has a direct impact on both strategic direction and operational efficiency, ultimately leading to improved overall performance.

- *H3: KM influences organizational performance.*
  - *H3a: Knowledge acquisition influences organizational performance.*
  - *H3b: Knowledge creation and generation influences organizational performance.*
  - *H3c: Knowledge utilization and application influences organizational performance.*
  - *H3d: Knowledge storing and updating influences organizational performance.*
  - *H3e: Knowledge Sharing and Transferring influences organizational performance.*
  - *H3f: Knowledge protection influences organizational performance.*

Finally, the fourth hypothesis emphasizes the mediating role of KM between ERP systems and organizational performance. This hypothesis suggests that KM acts as a mediator that enhances the role of ERP systems in improving organizational outcomes. The very logic of the connection lies in the fact that KM facilitates the dissemination of information throughout the organization, ensuring that insights derived from ERP data reach the right stakeholders in a usable form. This means that KM helps transform raw data from ERP systems into knowledge that supports informed strategic decisions and operational improvements. In this regard, Acar et al. (2017) discussing the relationship between ERP systems and organizational performance states that the impact of ERP use on operational performance is more pronounced when it is mediated by KM than through a direct effect only.

- *H4: KM mediates the relationship between ERP and organizational performance.*
  - *H4a: Knowledge acquisition mediates the relationship between ERP and organizational performance.*
  - *H4b: Knowledge creation and generation mediates the relationship between ERP and organizational performance.*
  - *H4c: Knowledge utilization and application mediates the relationship between ERP and organizational performance.*
  - *H4d: Knowledge storing and updating mediates the relationship between ERP and organizational performance.*
  - *H4e: Knowledge sharing and transferring mediates the relationship between ERP and organizational performance.*
  - *H4f: Knowledge protection mediates the relationship between ERP and organizational performance.*

5.3.2 Research Design

This study uses a quantitative research design to examine the impact of ERP and KM on organizational performance in Bosnia and Herzegovina (BiH). Primary data are collected through surveys using validated measurement scales for all variables, thus ensuring the reliability and validity of the data.

Survey participants are managers from a variety of industries, selected for their insights and valuable perspectives on the use of technology in organizational settings.

Measures for variables were derived from the scales established in previous research, and the panel of experts, by checking the nomological validity of the scales, confirmed that they are in accordance with the context of the research. The questionnaires were distributed electronically in the Bosnian language after the measurement indicators were translated from the original English language.

As in the previous example, structural equation modeling (SEM) will be used to analyze the data. SEM is ideal for testing complex models because it allows simultaneous analysis of multiple interdependent variables, combining factor analysis and multiple regression. This method provides a statistics comprehensive approach to examine the relationship between the theoretical frameworks established for this study.

5.3.3 Research Instrument

In order to conduct the study, a structured questionnaire was developed with closed questions that represented measurement indicators of the variables of interest. This questionnaire was built on existing works, and a seven-point Likert scale ranging from 1 (strongly disagree) to 7 (strongly agree) was used to assess participants' responses to the survey questions.

Additionally, the questionnaire incorporated a series of demographic questions aimed at collecting information about the respondents' backgrounds and the characteristics of their organizations.

The final questionnaire included measurement scales corresponding to each variable under investigation:

- Scale for ERP: To assess the effectiveness and integration of ERP systems within the organizational processes.
- Scale for KM—To assess the effectiveness and scope of knowledge management practices and their impact on organizational knowledge flow.
- Scale for organizational performance—To assess financial performance, this scale measures various financial indicators to gauge the overall financial health of the organization.

Below are the tables in which the indicators of the measurement scales are listed.

Table 5.19 shows a measurement scale for ERP with 3 dimensions: information quality, system quality and service quality. These items were rated on a Likert scale

Table 5.19 Measurement scale for the ERP

Dimension	Item code	Item
Information quality (InfQ)	InfQ1	The information provided by the ERP system is accurate
	InfQ2	Information from the ERP system is always timely
	InfQ3	The data provided by the ERP system is useful
	InfQ4	Information from the ERP system is easy to understand
	InfQ5	Importance of information related to decision-making
System quality (SysQ)	SysQ1	The ERP system is always up and running as necessary
	SysQ2	The ERP system responds quickly enough
	SysQ3	The ERP is easy to use
	SysQ4	The ERP user interface can be easily adapted to one's personal approach
Service quality (SerQ)	SerQ1	I receive prompt service from the IS department
	SerQ2	The information I receive from the IS department is accurate
	SerQ3	Training provided by the IS department improves my quality of work
	SerQ4	The IS department solves my problems
	SerQ5	The IS department delivers what they promise to deliver

ranging from 1 to 7, indicating agreement or disagreement. Indicators are taken from Ouiddad et al. (2020).

Table 5.20 presents a measuring scale for KM with 6 dimensions. Items were rated using a Likert scale ranging from 1 to 7, indicating a range of agreement or disagreement. This scale is taken from Tan and Wong (2015).

Table 5.20 Measurement scale for the KM

Dimension	Item code	Item
Knowledge acquisition (KAC)	KAC1	Employees acquire knowledge from customers or suppliers
	KAC2	Employees acquire knowledge from the company's knowledge repositories
Knowledge creation and generation (KCG)	KCG1	Employees create new knowledge, ideas, or solutions related to their tasks
	KCG2	Employees participate in brainstorming sessions to create new knowledge
	KCG3	Employees work in teams to create new knowledge
	KCG4	Rewards are given to employees who create new knowledge[a]
Knowledge utilization and application (KUA)	KUA1	Employees apply the best practices in their tasks
	KUA2	Employees apply knowledge from previous cases to solve problems
	KUA3	Employees apply the existing knowledge assets to generate value
	KUA4	Employees apply lesson's learnt from previous cases or experiences
Knowledge storing and updating (KSU)	KSU1	Employees spend time to codify and store knowledge in the company's knowledge repositories
	KSU2	Employees organize and classify knowledge for ease of retrieval
	KSU3	Employees update the stored knowledge
	KSU4	Employees are willing to contribute knowledge to the company's knowledge repositories
Knowledge sharing and transferring (KST)	KST1	Employees participate in meetings, discussions or other knowledge sharing activities
	KST2	Employees use technological tools (groupware, e-mails, networking tools, etc.) to share knowledge
	KST3	Mentorship is encouraged in the company
	KST4	Employees share knowledge through collaboration and interaction with each other
Knowledge protection (KP)	KP1	Knowledge is protected from loss
	KP2	Knowledge is protected from unauthorized access or being stolen
	KP3	Knowledge is protected via intellectual property rights
	KP4	Investment is given to protect knowledge

Table 5.21 Measurement scale for the organizational/business performance

Dimension	Item code	Item
Financial Performance (FP)	FP1	We have enhanced sales and profitability of the firm
	FP2	We have been profitable
	FP3	We have achieved profit objectives
	FP4	We have achieved sales objectives
	FP5	We have achieved market share objectives

Table 5.21 shows a scale of dimensions for an organization's financial performance. These items are rated using a Likert scale ranging from 1 to 7, indicating levels of disagreement or agreement. This scale was adapted from Chen et al. (2009).

5.3.4 Data Collection

These are key steps that were performed during the data collection process to test the set hypotheses and fulfil research aims and objectives; A wide range of sectors across Bosnia and Herzegovina were chosen, in view of the country's limited market size. Since the ERP systems are generally speaking universally applicable across different business sectors, all of them were analyzed.

In the primary stage of data gathering, a survey was designed which was based on an extensive literature search to develop measures for companies' capabilities in ERP and knowledge management, and how they influence business performance. For each construct, the most frequently used measurement scales were determined, and the appropriate ones were chosen for the study.

Following this, the questionnaire had been translated into Bosnian and put it into an online format using LimeSurvey software. Invitations to fill out the survey were sent by email with a link to go directly to online survey. The IT managers and CEOs of firms operating in Bosnia and Herzegovina because of their relevant expertise as well as roles within their organizations.

5.3.5 Sample

A convenience sample consists of 203 companies that reflect various industries and sizes. The way the sample was structured is briefly explained, focusing on the distribution in size and industry.

The sample spans three company sizes: small companies (35.86%), medium-sized ones (45.96%) and large firms (18.18%), as depicted in Table 5.22. This indicates the dominance of medium-sized enterprises, which may indicate their important role in the economy and perhaps greater agility and adaptability compared to large organizations. However, the extensive inclusion of both small and

Table 5.22 Sample size structure

Company size	%
Small	35.86
Medium	45.96
Large	18.18
Grand total	100.00

Table 5.23 Sample industry structure

Industry	%
Extraction of ores and stone	1.04
Manufacturing industry (production)	30.73
Water supply, wastewater removal, waste management and environmental rehabilitation activities	3.13
Construction	9.90
Wholesale and retail trade; repair of motor vehicles and motorcycles	21.35
Transportation and storage	5.21
Activities of providing accommodation and preparing and serving food (hotel and catering)	0.52
Information and communications	11.98
Financial activities and insurance activities	5.21
Real estate business	1.04
Professional, scientific and technical activities	3.13
Other service activities	6.77
(blank)	0.00
Grand total	100.00

large corporations guarantees different perspectives on the business and variables of interest.

Sample structure by industry is presented in Table 5.23. Manufacturing sector has the highest number of companies which is 30.73%. Wholesale and retail trade follows with 21.35% while information and communication take a third position at 11.98%. Furthermore, selected industries such as accommodation and food services, real estate show low representation rates as their figures stand at less than 1% (0.52%) and slightly above 1% (1.04%) respectively.

5.3.6 *Data Analysis and Results*

5.3.6.1 Evaluation of the Measurement Model

For data analysis, the same steps as for the analysis of the first model were followed. First, the measurement model was estimated and evaluated, and then the structural model was evaluated.

Table 5.24 Reliability and validity statistics of constructs

	Composite reliability (rho_a)	Composite reliability (rho_c)	Average variance extracted (AVE)
FP	0.911	0.922	0.705
InfQ	0.945	0.958	0.819
KAC	0.736	0.818	0.695
KCG	0.780	0.850	0.589
KP	0.918	0.920	0.743
KST	0.832	0.884	0.656
KSU	0.945	0.959	0.855
KUA	0.863	0.906	0.706
SerQ	0.921	0.939	0.754
SysQ	0.894	0.923	0.751

As noted earlier, reliability in PLS-SEM can be measured using composite reliability measures such as rho_a and rho_c. Both provide estimates of the internal consistency of the indicators measuring the latent construct. Although values above 0.6 may also be acceptable in exploratory research, the commonly agreed reliability threshold is 0.7 or higher. Strong reliabilities characterize all constructs with rho_a and rho_c values mostly exceeding the threshold value of 0.7, implying good internal consistency (presented in Table 5.24).

Furthermore, as shown in Table 5.25, each standardized loading exceeds the threshold of 0.7, thus confirming the convergent validity of the constructs within the measurement model. This shows that each indicator consistently measures its respective construct, thus ensuring that the constructs fairly reflect the variance resulting from the underlying theoretical propositions.

As a generally accepted method of assessing discriminant validity in models when PLS-SEM is used is the heterotrait-monotrait ratio (HTMT), where lower HTMT values indicate more pronounced differences between constructs. Table 5.26 shows that all constructs show good discriminant validity, that is, the HTMT ratios are below the threshold of 0.85, with the majority well below this threshold. For example, the construct pairs FP and InfQ, and FP and KP show HTMT ratios of 0.452 and 0.266, respectively, implying strong discriminant validity.

By comparing the square root of the average variance extracted (AVE) for each construct (diagonal values) with the correlations between the constructs (off-diagonal values), the Fornell-Larcker criterion is used to assess discriminant validity. Table 5.27 shows that, on most constructs, the square root of AVE, the value along the diagonal, is greater than its correlations with other constructs, indicating good discriminant validity. For the InfQ, the square root of the AVE is 0.905, for example, which exceeds its strongest correlation with any other construct, the SysQ, at 0.828. Similarly, with its AVE square root of 0.924, well above its correlations with other constructs, the KSU demonstrates fairly strong discriminant validity. These findings confirm that, in general, each construct is unique and captures elements not reflected by the others, which supports the reliability and specificity of the measurement model applied in the analysis.

Table 5.25 Convergent validity of constructs

	FP	InfQ	KAC	KCG	KP	KST	KSU	KUA	SerQ	SysQ
FP1	0.825									
FP2	0.814									
FP3	0.781									
FP4	0.908									
FP5	0.862									
InfQ1		0.927								
InfQ2		0.924								
InfQ3		0.894								
InfQ4		0.901								
InfQ5		0.877								
KAC1			0.728							
KAC2			0.927							
KCG1				0.776						
KCG2				0.749						
KCG3				0.874						
KCG4				0.656						
KP1					0.869					
KP2					0.896					
KP3					0.813					
KP4					0.867					
KST1						0.840				
KST2						0.731				
KST3						0.816				
KST4						0.847				
KSU1							0.911			
KSU2							0.933			
KSU3							0.948			
KSU4							0.905			
KUA1								0.828		
KUA2								0.847		
KUA3								0.878		
KUA4								0.808		
SerQ1									0.862	
SerQ2									0.883	
SerQ3									0.878	

After validating the measurement model, the structural model is tested. In order to understand the causal relationships within the proposed model, it is necessary to assess the interactions between the constructs. The power and relevance of important metrics including path coefficients, R-squared (R^2), effect sizes (f2) and predictive relevance (Q^2) will be assessed.

Table 5.26 Discriminant validity—Heterotrait-Monotrait (HTMT) ratio

	FP	InfQ	KAC	KCG	KP	KST	KSU	KUA	SerQ	SysQ
FP										
InfQ	0.452									
KAC	0.403	0.294								
KCG	0.293	0.329	0.680							
KP	0.266	0.204	0.528	0.605						
KST	0.398	0.388	0.491	0.765	0.649					
KSU	0.164	0.115	0.437	0.693	0.662	0.547				
KUA	0.397	0.379	0.508	0.836	0.497	0.803	0.645			
SerQ	0.395	0.697	0.235	0.322	0.273	0.387	0.206	0.382		
SysQ	0.361	0.899	0.283	0.402	0.303	0.413	0.271	0.461	0.741	

Note: Square root of AVE is on diagonal, and correlations are below

Table 5.27 Discriminant validity—Fornell-Larcker criterion

	FP	InfQ	KAC	KCG	KP	KST	KSU	KUA	SerQ	SysQ
FP	0.839									
InfQ	0.416	0.905								
KAC	0.317	0.240	0.833							
KCG	0.248	0.283	0.465	0.768						
KP	0.255	0.188	0.412	0.489	0.862					
KST	0.351	0.346	0.359	0.602	0.570	0.810				
KSU	0.160	0.109	0.348	0.588	0.622	0.484	0.924			
KUA	0.358	0.344	0.378	0.694	0.452	0.683	0.584	0.840		
SerQ	0.367	0.653	0.187	0.273	0.249	0.342	0.190	0.341	0.868	
SysQ	0.324	0.828	0.225	0.334	0.276	0.358	0.246	0.406	0.672	0.866

Note: Square root of AVE is on diagonal, and correlations are below

5.3.6.2 Evaluation of the Structural Model

As with previous model, Strategic ERP & KM synergy model is estimated, and results are presented below.

Strategic ERP & KM synergy, as presented in Fig. 5.7 and grounded in DCV offers a comprehensive overview of how ERP and KM contribute to organizational financial performance.

The results of the proposed model evaluation are presented in Table 5.28. Supported by the data ($\beta = 0.243$; $t = 2.580$; $p = 0.010$), the first hypothesis, H1a, posits a strong positive impact of the ERP system on knowledge acquisition (KAC). This result highlights how ERP systems help improve the capacity to acquire knowledge from many sources, including internal repositories, suppliers, and consumers. On the other hand, H1b investigated the impact of ERP on knowledge creation and generation (KCG) within the organization and revealed a stronger and statistically significant relationship ($\beta = 0.328$; $t = 4.754$; $p = 0.001$), which indicates that ERP

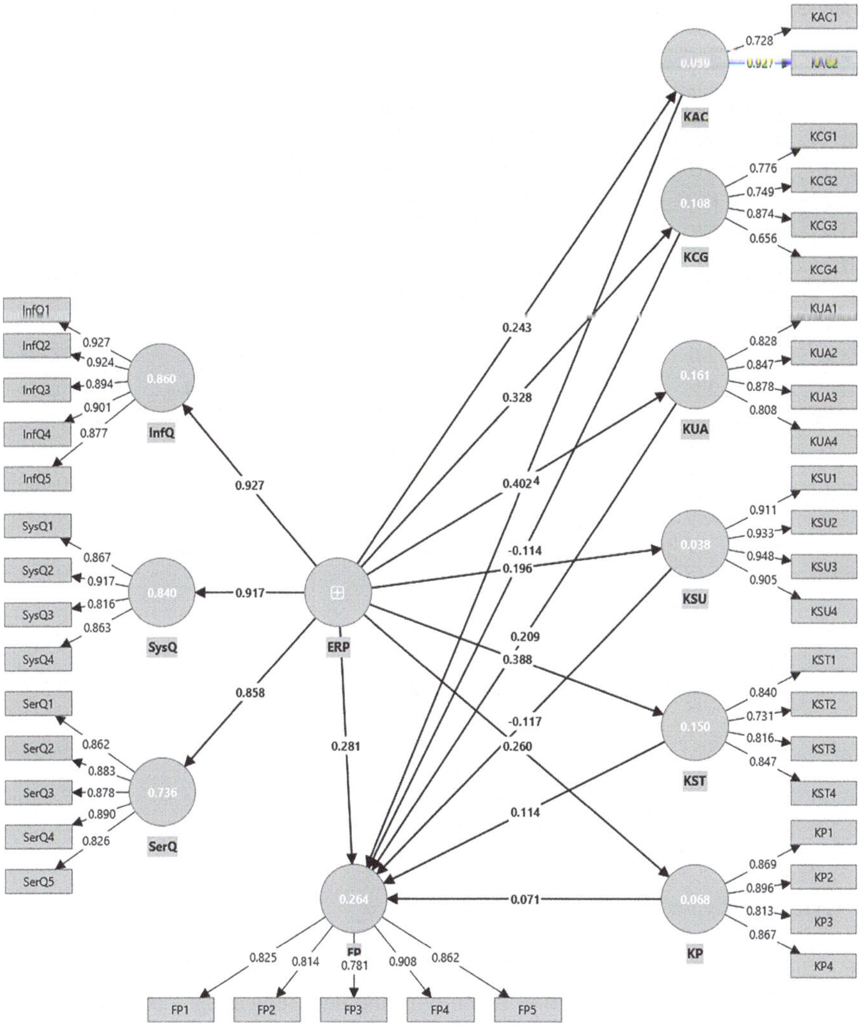

Fig. 5.7 Strategic ERP & KM synergy model

systems are particularly successful in creating an environment that promotes knowledge creation through teamwork and brainstorming.

H1c targeting the impact of ERP on knowledge use and application (KUA), the effect was even more clearly positive ($\beta = 0.402$; $t = 5.227$; $p = 0.001$). This implies that ERP systems greatly assist in applying best practices and using past experiences to solve problems and create value. Presenting a positive effect ($\beta = 0.196$; $t = 2.715$; $p = 0.007$), H1d assessed the effect of ERP on knowledge storage and updating (KSU). This suggests that ERP systems support the organization and updating of knowledge within corporate repositories.

Table 5.28 Structural model evaluation

		Original sample (O)	Sample mean (M)	Standard deviation (STDEV)	T statistics (|O/STDEV|)	P values
H1a	ERP → KAC	0.243	0.252	0.094	2.580	0.010
H1b	ERP → KCG	0.328	0.344	0.069	4.754	0.000
H1c	ERP → KUA	0.402	0.408	0.077	5.223	0.000
H1d	ERP → KSU	0.196	0.204	0.072	2.715	0.007
H1e	ERP → KST	0.388	0.397	0.096	4.019	0.000
H1f	ERP → KP	0.260	0.271	0.078	3.354	0.001
H2	ERP → FP	0.282	0.294	0.082	3.461	0.001
H3a	KAC → FP	0.193	0.195	0.096	2.004	0.045
H3b	KCG → FP	−0.112	−0.096	0.086	1.295	0.195
H3c	KUA → FP	0.209	0.198	0.100	2.094	0.036
H3d	KST → FP	0.113	0.097	0.086	1.305	0.192
H3e	KSU → FP	−0.119	−0.123	0.081	1.467	0.142
H3f	KP → FP	0.071	0.080	0.097	0.729	0.466
H4a	ERP → KAC → FP	0.047	0.048	0.031	1.517	0.129
H4b	ERP → KCG → FP	−0.037	−0.033	0.031	1.190	0.234
H4c	ERP → KUA → FP	0.084	0.081	0.044	1.898	0.058
H4d	ERP → KSU → FP	−0.023	−0.024	0.019	1.245	0.213
H4e	ERP → KST → FP	0.044	0.036	0.035	1.260	0.208
H4f	ERP → KP → FP	0.018	0.020	0.027	0.675	0.500

H1e investigated how ERP affected knowledge sharing and transfer (KST) and also found a significant positive effect ($\beta = 0.388$; $t = 4.019$; $p = 0.001$), implying that ERP uses different tools to help knowledge sharing. H1f examined the impact of ERP on knowledge protection (KP), with the data indicating a positive impact ($\beta = 0.260$; $t = 3.354$; $p = 0.001$), thus indicating that ERP systems help protect knowledge from loss or illegal access.

Furthermore, strongly supported by the results ($\beta = 0.282$; $t = 3.461$; $p = 0.001$), hypothesis H2 suggests that ERP directly increases firm performance (FP). This suggests that the strategic integration of ERP systems can greatly improve the overall performance of an enterprise.

With $\beta = 0.193$; $t = 2.004$; $p = 0.045$, H3a shows that the ability to acquire knowledge from many sources directly improves firm performance. On company performance, however, the creation and generation of knowledge shows a negative impact ($\beta = -0.112$; $t = 1.295$; $p = 0.195$), which is not statistically significant and suggests that this relationship may be complicated or influenced by other factors that are not covered by this model. H3c shows the need for proper use of knowledge in improving company results, showing a positive and significant effect of the use and application of knowledge on company performance (β = 0.209; t = 2.094; p = 0.036). Suggesting possible problems in knowledge sharing and storage mechanisms that do not translate directly into improved performance, H3d and H3e show an insignificant and somewhat negative impact on firm performance (H3d: β = 0.113; t = 1.305; p = 0.192, H3e: β = – 0.119; t = 1.467; H3f, looking at how knowledge protection affects company performance, also shows a weak and insignificant positive impact (β = 0.071; t = 0.466).

The results of testing H4a suggest that there is no mediating role of KAC (β = 0.047; t = 1.517; p = 0.129) between ERP and organizational performance. H4b even shows a smaller negative mediation effect (β = −0.037; t = 1.190; p = 0.234), suggesting once again that ERP may not be able to improve performance through knowledge generation. With β = 0.084; t = 1.898; p = 0.058, H4c shows a noticeable mediation effect suggesting a possible positive role of KUA in enabling ERP to increase firm performance. Both H4d and H4e show rather weak and insignificant mediation effects (H4d: β = −0.023; t = 1.245; p = 0.213, H4e: β = 0.044; t = 1.260; p = 0.208), i.e. that knowledge storing and updating, as and knowledge sharing and transferring are not mediators of the relationship between ERP and the firm's financial performance. Among the tested hypotheses, H4f shows the lowest mediation effect (β = 0.018; t = 0.675; p = 0.500), which indicates that there is no mediation effect of knowledge protection practices between ERP and company performance.

The R^2 values from the structural model offer a complex picture of how effectively the predictors explain the variance in each endogenous variable in the study of ERP systems and knowledge management and their effects on organizational performance. The R^2 values are presented in Table 5.29. The R^2 value of 0.237 for FP shows that the effects of ERP and several knowledge practices—knowledge acquisition, creation, use, sharing, storage, and protection—explain about 23.7% of the variance in company performance. This value implies that, although knowledge practices and the ERP system clearly influence firm performance, other important influencing elements are not adequately reflected in this model. However, it is important to note that this level of R2 was also considered adequate in social research. With a rather low R2 value of 0.054, the KAC indicates that the predictors, mainly the ERP system, help explain only 5.4% of the variance in how effectively employees acquire knowledge. This implies that the current model does not include other external or internal elements that clearly influence knowledge acquisition.

Table 5.29 Coefficients of determination (R^2)

	R-square	R-square adjusted
FP	0.264	0.237
KAC	0.059	0.054
KCG	0.108	0.103
KP	0.068	0.063
KST	0.150	0.146
KSU	0.038	0.034
KUA	0.161	0.157

With an R^2 value of 0.103, the model explains approximately 10.3% of the variance of KCG. This value suggests that ERP systems help to some degree in knowledge creation, but most of the variation in KCG is caused by elements outside our current focus. KP, with an R^2 value of 0.063, also shows that the model explains 6.3% of how knowledge is protected within companies. With an R^2 value of 0.146, KST has a rather better explanatory power, which means that the model explains approximately 14.6% of the variance in knowledge sharing and knowledge transfer practices. This indicates the impact of ERP systems on enabling knowledge sharing through shared environments and technical tools. With an R^2 value of 0.034 KSU shows the lowest level of explained variance. This value highlights that the model explains little of the variance in KSU, indicating a significant difference in the model elements related to knowledge storage and updating. Finally, the KUA shows an R^2 value of 0.157, implying that ERP systems help explain approximately 15.7% of the variance in knowledge application in organizational processes. This suggests a reasonable influence, but also allows room for other elements, such as personal capacity and organizational environment, to be considered in subsequent investigations.

Assuming all other variables are held constant, the effect sizes f^2 shown in Table 5.30 help understand the impact of ERP on different knowledge management practices and performance outcomes by quantifying the change of one variable over another. ERP has a mean effect size of 0.193 for KUA, which reflects the significant impact of ERP on the degree of application and use of knowledge within the company. With an effect size of 0.177, ERP on KST suggests a fairly strong impact on improving the mechanisms and channels of knowledge exchange and transfer among employees. Both ERP on KCG with an effect size of 0.12 and KP with 0.073 both show a modest impact, implying that although ERP helps these practices, its impact is not as strong as on the previous two practices. ERP on KAC and FP reveal smaller effect sizes of 0.063 and 0.086.

With a small effect size of 0.037, KAC on FP shows that knowledge acquisition has some effect on company performance. Taken alone, other knowledge

Table 5.30 f^2 effect sizes

	FP	InfQ	KAC	KCG	KP	KST	KSU	KUA	SerQ	SysQ
ERP	0.086	6.149	0.063	0.12	0.073	0.177	0.04	0.193	2.781	5.258
FP										
InfQ										
KAC	0.037									
KCG	0.007									
KP	0.003									
KST	0.007									
KSU	0.009									
KUA	0.022									
SerQ										
SysQ										

Table 5.31 Predictive relevance (Q^2)

	Q^2	RMSE	MAE
FP	0.139	0.946	0.652
InfQ	0.866	0.382	0.276
KAC	0.032	1.015	0.689
KCG	0.072	0.987	0.728
KP	0.040	0.998	0.701
KST	0.100	0.967	0.680
KSU	0.013	1.013	0.694
KUA	0.121	0.951	0.694
SerQ	0.743	0.526	0.363
SysQ	0.840	0.413	0.303

dimensions including KCG, KP, KST, KSU and KUA on FP show rather small effect sizes (ranging from 0.003 to 0.227), implying small effects on firm performance.

The results shown in Table 5.31 regarding the predictive relevance (Q^2), root mean square error (RMSE) and mean absolute error (MAE) provide an analysis of the performance of the structural model within the PLS-SEM framework. These tests assess the predictive and explanatory ability of the model for each endogenous construct. Given that all values are positive, it can be concluded that the model has predictive ability.

With lower Q^2 values of 0.032 and 0.013, respectively, KAC and KSU show that the model has some predictive power for these dimensions. Although not as much, other knowledge-related dimensions, including KCG, KP, and KUA, show fairly low Q^2 values, indicating some predictive relevance. Firm performance (FP) has a Q^2 value of 0.139, which confirms the presence of predictive relevance. This shows that the model can somewhat consistently predict the impact of ERP systems on firm performance. However, as is common in social studies, the accuracy of the predictions is mostly average, and it is mostly possible to improve the model by including additional variables. However, the aim of this study was to analyze the relationships between ERP, KM and organizational performance, without the need for a clear prediction.

5.3.6.3 Discussion of the Results

The strategic ERP & KM synergy model provides a complex exploration of the interactions between ERP systems and KM practices and their combined impact on company performance. Combining organizational culture with technical environment, i.e. elements of quality related to ERP, this study provides a thorough framework for understanding several aspects of the effects of technology in companies.

The model shows a significant direct impact of the ERP system on several knowledge management practices. With corresponding t-values of 4.754 and 5.227, ERP clearly affects knowledge creation and generation (KCG) as well as knowledge use and application (KUA), so that supporting environments that enhance knowledge creation and effective use are greatly enhanced by ERP systems. Additionally, the observed positive effects are shown by knowledge exchange and transfer (KST) and knowledge protection (KP), which highlights the role of ERP in enabling knowledge distribution and preservation within the company. On the other hand, knowledge acquisition (KAC) and knowledge storage and updating (KSU) show smaller but still significant positive effects, which implies different impact of ERP on several levels of KM.

With a t-value of 3.461, the strategic ERP & KM synergy model shows even a direct positive impact of ERP on firm performance (FP), thus highlighting the important part of ERP in improving organizational performance through simplified processes and better efficiency.

Several theoretical implications arising from the interaction between the dimensions of knowledge management and organizational performance have been extensively explored, thus advancing the understanding of knowledge as a strategic tool in companies. Knowledge acquisition is assumed to improve financial performance. This can be theoretically explained by the theory that companies that actively seek and absorb fresh knowledge are more apt to be creative and flexible enough to respond to changing market conditions. This alignment with dynamic capabilities theory implies that competitive advantage is driven by the ability to translate acquired knowledge into operational excellence, thereby improving financial performance. On the other hand, less clear conclusions have been drawn about how knowledge generation affects financial performance. Although building knowledge assets is important, it is assumed that increasing these assets alone does not lead directly to better financial performance. Resource-based theory can help explain this result because it emphasizes not only the acquisition of invaluable resources but also their efficient use. The negative relationship explored could represent the overhead associated with handling significant amounts of knowledge that may not yet be fully exploited for financial advantage.

Furthermore, supporting a theoretical framework that emphasizes the practical application of knowledge as a fundamental determinant of organizational success is the part that the use of knowledge plays in influencing financial performance. This is in line with DCV according to which the deliberate application of existing knowledge can result in innovation and efficiency improvements strengthening the company's financial situation.

The model also estimates indirect effects between ERP implementation and company performance, i.e. the mediating relationship of KM practices. These results are contradictory; some paths, such as ERP → KAC → FP, show fewer mediating effects, while others, such as ERP → KUA → FP, show more interesting but still insignificant effects. This variability implies that although ERP can improve KM practices, its indirect effect on company performance through these practices may not be as significant, suggesting possible areas for more research and model improvement including variables between ERP and KM, or between KM and organizational performance.

5.3.6.4 Research Limitations

Examining the impact of ERP system implementation on company performance, the conducted research revealed several limitations and offers suggestions for further research on this matter. The operationalization of the measurement scales could have affected the depth and breadth of the results. In subsequent research, changes or extensions of these scales may offer more complex knowledge about the impacts of ERP. Certain research limitations during data collection could have affected the representativeness and comprehensiveness of the data. Greater generalizability of the results depends on more diverse data collection techniques, so future studies could benefit from them. The interpretation of the ERP system's impact on the organization's performance may have suffered from shortcomings in the analytical approaches used. Using more diverse analytical approaches could reveal a deeper understanding and support the conclusions drawn.

Based on a sample of companies from Bosnia and Herzegovina, the findings of the study indicate possible general relevance for neighboring nations. But given that most of the respondents were either CEOs or IT managers of small, medium and large enterprises, these direct decision makers and participants in ERP implementation provide a unique perspective.

Future studies should cover managers from other business sectors. ERP systems by nature connect important business areas, so management at all levels must have fundamental knowledge. Along with diversifying the spectrum of insights, this growth would improve knowledge about the effects of ERP across many levels of management and functional sectors.

Future research can build on the fundamental insights provided by the strategic ERP & KM synergy model by addressing limitations and expanding the scope of research, thus contributing to a stronger and more complete framework for understanding the strategic integration of ERP systems in improving organizational performance and knowledge. Management practices.

5.3.7 Conclusion

This study proposes a strategic ERP & KM synergy model consisting of 4 hypotheses and multiple hypotheses that assess the various interactions between enterprise resource planning (ERP) systems and various knowledge management (KM) practices within companies, thus highlighting their combined impact on company performance. Including both technical and organizational aspects that influence the efficiency of ERP, this model improves knowledge about its adoption and interaction with KM systems.

The model suggests that ERP systems greatly improve some important aspects of knowledge management. The observed direct effects, such as the significant impact of ERP on the creation and generation of knowledge (KCG) and the use and application of knowledge (KUA), show that ERP systems are necessary in creating an environment suitable for innovation and efficient application of knowledge. Likewise, the favorable impact on knowledge exchange and transfer (KST) and knowledge protection (KP) underlines the role of ERP in enabling knowledge distribution and security within companies.

Moreover, the model clarifies a direct positive relationship between ERP systems and company performance implying that ERP adoption can result in better operational efficiency and organizational results. This is particularly important because it offers real evidence for the strategic integration of ERP systems in promoting organizational success.

Regarding the direct links between knowledge management practices and organizational performance, the model supports the impact of knowledge acquisition and knowledge application on organizational performance. Other practices, including knowledge creation and generation, knowledge storage and updating, knowledge exchange and transfer, and knowledge protection do not show a significant impact on financial performance. Practically, this suggests that companies could gain more by concentrating their efforts on properly acquiring external knowledge and using that knowledge strategically in their activities.

This result implies that the value of knowledge management practices is not only in the acquisition or possession of knowledge, but mainly in the application of knowledge to achieve visible results. For example, even if knowledge creation is fundamental, its ability to improve performance may be limited without strong systems for properly implementing this knowledge in innovation or decision-making processes.

Similarly, the limited impact of storing, updating, sharing and protecting knowledge on current financial performance could reflect the more complex value of these practices, which may contribute to long-term sustainability and resilience rather than immediate financial gains. Organizations seeking quick returns may therefore give top priority to developing competencies related to acquiring relevant markets and using them for operational or strategic benefits from competitive intelligence.

Practically, managers should take care to transfer funds to improve systems and procedures that enable efficient acquisition and application of knowledge. This strategic emphasis can help improve organizational skills directly related to competitive advantage and better financial performance. Furthermore, even if their direct financial impact seems small, other knowledge-based practices are absolutely necessary to develop an informed and agile organizational culture that can support long-term success.

However, mixed results are shown when it comes to the mediation effects that the model explores, those between ERP and firm performance through different knowledge management practices. Although some routes show possible influence, others are less strong, implying the complexity of ERP's function in organizational dynamics. These results inspire more research on how ERP systems could be more closely aligned with KM techniques to maximize company performance.

The proposed strategic ERP & KM synergy model, as presented in Fig. 5.8, offers a whole framework that emphasizes the important combination of ERP and

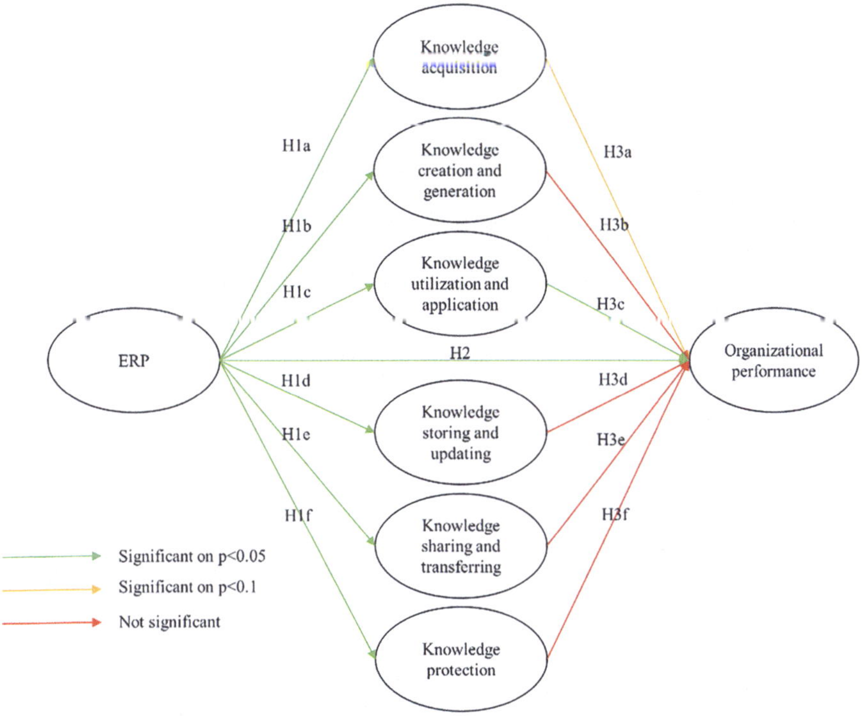

Fig. 5.8 Strategic ERP & KM synergy model

knowledge management in companies. It emphasizes the need to use technology and develop organizational cultures that help the acquisition and application of knowledge. Future studies should continue to explore this dynamic, perhaps expanding the model to include other factors that influence the adoption and effectiveness of ERP in different corporate environments, and that possibly lie between ERP and KM, or between KM and business performance. Nevertheless, this research through the two models offered offers empirical evidence to organizations hoping to fully utilize ERP systems by convincing them that these systems contribute to maximizing the effectiveness of knowledge management and influence the overall performance of the firm.

References

Abugabah, A., Sanzogni, L., & Alfarraj, O. (2015). Evaluating the impact of ERP systems in higher education. *International Journal of Information and Learning Technology, 32*(1), 45–64. https://doi.org/10.1108/IJILT-10-2013-0058

Acar, M. F., Tarim, M., Zaim, H., Zaim, S., & Delen, D. (2017). Knowledge management and ERP: Complementary or contradictory? *International Journal of Information Management, 37*(6), 703–712. https://doi.org/10.1016/j.ijinfomgt.2017.05.007

Anderson, J. C., & Gerbing, D. W. (1988). Structural equation modeling in practice : A review and recommended two-step approach. *Psychological Bulletin, 103*(3), 411–423.
Chen, L., & Fong, P. S. W. (2012). Revealing performance heterogeneity through knowledge management maturity evaluation: A capability-based approach. *Expert Systems with Applications, 39*(18), 13523–13539. https://doi.org/10.1016/j.eswa.2012.07.005
Chen, J. S., Tsou, H. T., & Huang, A. Y. H. (2009). Service delivery innovation: Antecedents and impact on firm performance. *Journal of Service Research, 12*(1), 36–55. https://doi.org/10.1177/1094670509338619
Cohen, J. (1988). *Statistical power analysis for the behavioral sciences*. Lawrence Erlbaum Associates.
Davis, F. (1989). Perceived usefulness, perceived ease of use, and user acceptance of information technology. *MIS Quarterly, 13*(3), 319–340.
Davis, F. D., & Venkatesh, V. (1996). A critical assessment of potential measurement biases in the technology acceptance model : Three experiments. *International Journal of Human-Computer Studies, 45*(1), 19–45.
Erasmus, E., Rothmann, S., & van Eeden, C. (2015). A structural model of technology acceptance. *SA Journal of Industrial Psychology, 41*(1). https://doi.org/10.4102/sajip.v41i1.1222
Gumussoy, C. A., Calisir, F., & Bayram, A. (2007). Understanding the behavioral intention to use ERP systems: An extended technology acceptance model. IEEM 2007: 2007 IEEE international conference on industrial engineering and engineering management, 2024–2028. https://doi.org/10.1109/IEEM.2007.4419547
Hair, J. F. Jr., Hult, T. G. M., Ringle, C. M., & Sarstedt, M. (2014). A primer on partial least squares structural equation modeling (PLS-SEM). In *Long range planning* (Vol. 46, Issues 1–2). Sage. https://doi.org/10.1016/j.lrp.2013.01.002
Hair, J. F. J., Black, W. C., Babin, B. J., & Anderson, R. E. (2019). *Multivariate data analysis*. Cengage Learning EMEA. https://doi.org/10.1002/9781119409137.ch4
Helfat, C. E., & Peteraf, M. A. (2009). Understanding dynamic capabilities: Progress along a developmental path. *Strategic Organization, 7*(1), 91–102. https://doi.org/10.1177/1476127008100133
Ike Wahyuning, W., Lubis, M., Witjaksono, W., & Azizah, A. H. (2019, November 1). Implementation of Enterprise resource planning (ERP) using integrated model of extended technology acceptance model (TAM) 2: Case study of PT. Toyota Astra Motor. *2019 7th international conference on cyber and IT service management*, CITSM 2019. https://doi.org/10.1109/CITSM47753.2019.8965342
Imam, H., & Zaheer, M. K. (2021). Shared leadership and project success: The roles of knowledge sharing, cohesion and trust in the team. *International Journal of Project Management, 39*(5), 463–473.
Kuo, R. Z., & Lee, G. G. (2009). KMS adoption: The effects of information quality. *Management Decision, 47*(10), 1633–1651. https://doi.org/10.1108/00251740911004727
Lin, C. S., & Wu, S. (2002). *Exploring the impact of online service quality on portal site usage*. www.yam.com.tw
Metaxiotis, K. (2009). Exploring the rationales for ERP and knowledge management integration in SMEs. *Journal of Enterprise Information Management, 22*(1–2), 51–62. https://doi.org/10.1108/17410390910922822
Ouiddad, A., Okar, C., Chroqui, R., & Beqqali Hassani, I. (2020). Assessing the impact of enterprise resource planning on decision-making quality: An empirical study. *Kybernetes, 50*, 1144–1162. https://doi.org/10.1108/K-04-2019-0273
Salloum, S. A., Al-Emran, M., & Shaalan, K. (2018). The impact of knowledge sharing on information systems: A review. *Communications in Computer and Information Science, 877*, 94–106. https://doi.org/10.1007/978-3-319-95204-8_9
Sedera, D., & Gable, G. G. (2010). Knowledge management competence for enterprise system success. *Journal of Strategic Information Systems, 19*(4), 296–306. https://doi.org/10.1016/j.jsis.2010.10.001

Shivers-Blackwell, S. L., & Charles, A. C. (2006). Ready, set, go: Examining student readiness to use ERP technology. *Journal of Management Development, 25*(8), 795–805. https://doi.org/10.1108/02621710610684268

Tan, L. P., & Wong, K. Y. (2015). Linkage between knowledge management and manufacturing performance: A structural equation modeling approach. *Journal of Knowledge Management, 19*(4), 814–835. https://doi.org/10.1108/JKM-11-2014-0487

Teece, D. J., Pisano, G., & Shuen, A. (1997). Dynamic capabilities and strategic management: Organizing for innovation and growth. *Strategic Management Journal, 18*(7), 509–533. http://scholar.google.com/scholar?hl=en&btnG=Search&q=intitle:Dynamic+capabilities+and+strategic+management:+organizing+for+innovation+and+growth#0

Venkatesh, V., & Goyal, S. (2010). Expectation disconfirmation and technology adoption: Polynomial modeling and response surface analysis. *MIS Quarterly Management Information Systems, 34*(SPEC. ISSUE 2), 281–303. https://doi.org/10.2307/20721428

Index

L. Turulja et al., *Integrating ERP Systems and Knowledge Management*, Progress in IS, https://doi.org/10.1007/978-3-031-68922-2

The manufacturer's authorised representative in the EU is Springer
Nature Customer Service Centre GmbH, Europaplatz 3, 69115 Heidelberg,
Germany. If you have any concerns regarding our products, please
contact ProductSafety@springernature.com

Printed and bound by CPI Group (UK) Ltd, Croydon, CR0 4YY
30/09/2026
02225607-0014